HOW MANY DOGS?!

How Many Dogs?!

Using Positive Reinforcement Training to Manage a Multiple Dog Household

Debby McMullen, CDBC

Published by Tanacacia Press
6127 PA Route 873
Slatington, PA 18080
610 570-9039

For general information on Debby McMullen or Pawsitive Reactions LLC., go to www.pawsitivereactions.com, call 412-766-7632, or email debby@pawsitivereactions.com.

ISBN 13: 978-0-9766414-2-1

Cover Design: Stacey Ziegler, Pete Smoyer, and Debby McMullen
Book Design: Pete Smoyer, e-Production
Cover photographs by: Babeth Raible

Manufactured in the United States of America

This book is dedicated first and foremost to my own crew—Merlin, Kera, Siri & Trent—who have been patient with my failings and loved me all the same.

And to crews of dogs still waiting in rescues and shelters for forever homes. Adopt and save a life. You will learn more than you ever dreamed possible.

Table of Contents

Chapter 1

Becoming the Crew Leader!
The Basics of Living with Multiple Dogs

Do you enjoy (or at least tolerate) living in chaos? Do you have more leashes and collars than underwear? Do you have the vet, groomer and pet supply store on speed dial? Do you plan your wardrobe around which dog activity you are participating in that day? Then this is the book for you! It takes a special kind of person to go past that two-dog mark and even more of an adventurous spirit to go beyond that. But it can be done and it can be done not only successfully but happily and you may never want to go back. Your life will have more limits, but it will also have more rewards. Those rewards come in the way of sloppy kisses and wagging tails, but rewards they are all the same.

You do not need a large house to have multiple dogs, but I would be lying if I said it doesn't help. Securely fenced yards are worth their weight in gold, but again, all you really need is energy and determination. So are you ready to jump in with all four paws? Let's delve into the world of the multiple dog household and see what you might be getting into. Either you currently have multiple dogs or you are thinking about entering that world. Whichever describes your current situation, you've come to the right place.

If you already have multiple dogs, do you have calm or chaos when you are all just hanging around the house? Do you have a combination and wish it were more calm than chaos? Do your dogs wrestle and roughhouse inside when you'd rather they do so outside? This would be a good time to start training of course, but you also need to integrate some new behaviors into your dogs' daily lives. Like a good parent guides his/her children in the right direction, so shall you situate yourself into this very same role. But rather than considering yourself a parent to your dog, I'd like to introduce you to the concept of the benevolent leader.

Establishing Benevolent Leadership

When living with multiple dogs, or even a single dog for that matter, remember that you are the "GIVER OF ALL GOOD THINGS". Establish yourself in this role with your dogs and you will be able to retain the role of guidance giver. By establishing yourself as a benevolent leader, you will find that everything will flow more smoothly. A benevolent leader is like a parent whose children never grow up. You set guidelines and limits and teach your crew that good behavior gets lots of rewards. Good leadership is not about correcting or punishing bad behavior. When your crew thinks that all good things come from you, they look to you for direction. They don't worry so much about things out in the world that might be scary. They trust in you to keep them safe. They trust in you to keep them fed, warm and housed. It all flows from these concepts.

> If you'd like to train the behaviors first and then read about how to apply them, please skip straight to the last chapter, Proofing the Pups. We all learn differently so do whatever works best for you!

Leadership can be taken to levels that are too strict. I am not an advocate of a strict "Nothing in Life is Free" program. This entails too much control. Total control is not a fun concept. It is not necessary to rule with an iron grip. Life with your dog should not be like a boot camp. Creating a standoff can result in a break in trust and unnecessary tension. I am here to teach you to be a loving leader. This book is all about rewarding the behavior you like and redirecting the behavior you don't like. Teaching your dogs to ask politely for what they want teaches them that they can control the outcome of a situation. This creates a partnership between you and your dogs. This concept is explained more fully in the Proofing the Pups chapter, in the section on capturing. It's a win/win situation that makes for an eager to please dog.

Do not fall into the trap of thinking about alpha dogs and beta dogs. Throw out those words. Throw out any notions of dominance.

It is not your job to dominate your dogs, nor to let them dominate each other. It's all about benevolence. You are the benevolent leader. You are the one with the opposable thumbs. You are in charge, like a loving parent. However, that fact does not make you the alpha dog. You are the human. Your dogs know that you are a different species than they are, and they fully appreciate that feature. They do not need you to communicate with them like an alpha wolf supposedly does with his subordinates; this is a widely held but inaccurate understanding of an alpha wolf's relationship with his subordinates. Throw that idea right out the window. Never look back!

Truthfully, the alpha wolf in nature is a benevolent leader, never needing to use violence to communicate. They share their resources and they understand that everyone works together. True leaders do not push and shove. There is no need to force anyone to do anything.

> Benevolent Leadership is about placing yourself in the position of being looked to for direction. It is about setting appropriate limits and guidelines so that your dogs know what is expected of them. It is about trust that you will take care of things.

Leaders earn respect by leading well. Leaders have presence and confidence. Like the subordinate wolves, your dogs need your benevolent leadership. They need and want to look to you for direction and limits. They want to respect your decision making. Dogs LIKE limits and most will easily respect the limits that you set forth for them when you use these limits effectively and enforce them consistently.

And enforce them you should, but with kindness and respect. You are not meant to rule with an iron fist. Or a jerking leash! Your leadership will be respected most when your dogs enjoy looking to you for direction. You can make compliance with your wishes the most fun experience in the universe for your dogs. You know how to speak human language; your dogs know how to speak dog. It's up to you to learn how to effectively communicate with them, in order to smoothly lead a multiple dog household. Do not leave the dogs to "work things out amongst themselves." That could be disastrous! Think fur flying, furniture damaged — oh, the possibilities are endless.

When your dogs have their basic needs fulfilled by you on a regular basis, they learn to trust in you as the supreme provider of all good things. This trust is the key to being a successful benevolent leader. Dogs like to know that they have a basic routine they can trust. This helps to build the foundation for a calmer dog.

Do you always have to step in? Of course not! But you must always have an eye open to what is going on in a multiple dog household, whether long-established or a brand new mix of dogs. You may have to step in to redirect inappropriate behavior. When you have an established crew in your house, life gets easier as routines become second nature. Your eyes and instincts will almost always tell you when you must pay extra attention.

But when first integrating a crew, it's necessary to exercise 24/7 observation; especially if you are also a rescuer and take different dogs into your home on a regular basis. Some rescuers never mix in the foster dogs with their own dogs. I personally do because I think it not only helps my own dogs to be better socialized, but it also helps the foster dogs learn to utilize the manners required to live in a high energy household with many personalities. This is a win/win situation in my book.

How do my dogs like this choice? It goes back to trust. Trust in you and your benevolent leadership is the key to successfully managing a multiple dog household. While starting to write this book, I fostered five puppies that I took in when they were ten weeks old. My dogs were not terribly happy about this development at first, but they take these things in stride. They trust me to make sure that their needs are still met and that I will keep them safe from puppy annoyances as needed. I trust them not to hurt any foster dog, including delicate puppies.

We have raised several litters of puppies in this house. Since my dog Siri, came from one of those litters, I thought this would be an okay thing to agree to. So if you foster dogs and have a multiple dog household, it's important to try to keep in mind what your workload and energy level may be. Also remember that your ability to manage multiple dogs can differ at different times in your life.

I have learned that one can bite off more than one can chew. While my dogs wanted for almost nothing during this period, *almost* is the key word. They did get less personal attention. Remember that your own crew should always come first. If having too many dogs creates too much stress in your life, then you damage the trusting relationship with your dogs that you've worked so hard to achieve. Trust certainly can be restored, but preventing the break in trust in the first place is the best option. Staying within the number of dogs you can comfortably take good care of is an important consideration.

Of course, like me, many of you will learn by experience how many is too many. Make sure that once you experience that point, you learn from that experience. The trust between you and your dogs is very important! Another very important thing to keep in mind is how you handle stress. If

> Know your limits: stick with the quantity of dogs that you can comfortably provide for in all aspects of the meaning of the word. To push your limits sets the stage for stress in you and your crew.

you travel much past your threshold, you can become too stressed to be a good dog mom or dad. Try not to travel past it with too many dogs. Remember, you are not the only person who can love and care for dogs, so you don't need to have them all. Stick to the amount that you are comfortable with.

So how do you develop that ever important trust? That is an intricate answer. Trust is relationship-based. Trust in your leadership means that your dogs have learned that you can and will keep them safe from harm and take care of any threats. Trust means that you will provide for their basic needs, such as food, water, exercise, comfort, bathroom needs, etc. Trust means that they have a schedule that is maintained predictably most of the time, especially for the aforementioned basics. And when the schedule is off a bit, your dogs will go with the flow because of that trust.

Trust, to me, is love expanded. Trust is the ultimate form of love. You develop trust by developing your relationship with your dogs. Do you communicate with your dogs or do you talk at them? If you truly communicate with them, you know how trust feels. They look at you with trust. They check

> Positive (reward) training is the scientifically based method of training an animal by rewarding the behavior that you want and ignoring or redirecting the behavior that you don't want.

in with you frequently. They enjoy connecting with you. It's there to see.

Let's talk about how to establish benevolent leadership and trust. Doing so will help you carve calm out of chaos. Benevolent leadership will also help you to teach your dogs what is expected of them. It will help you set limits and establish a routine. My approach is based on positive reinforcement training and a hands-off approach. You will not find any force training techniques in here. Since this is not intended to be a complete step-by-step dog training manual, I will not be going into intricate explanations of positive training. I am going to make the assumption that if you don't already have some basic understanding of this method of training, that you will read more on the subject if my explanations are not sufficient.

You will find some basics of positive training covered in the Proofing the Pups chapter, as well as some step-by-step directions for various training cues. However, the more you can read on this subject, the better understanding you will have of what I will cover in this book. There are some excellent books named in the reference section covering both the basics and specific needs. I urge you to avail yourself of their knowledge.

A marker word is a word spoken to mark or capture the exact instant your dog does the desired behavior. A clicker is a small box shaped device that makes a sound that is distinctive. It functions as an impartial and high value marker. Marking the moment that your dog does something that you like is something that would be very beneficial for you as the crew leader to become very good at!

You will need to learn how to use either a marker word or a clicker, or preferably both. One of the most important terms in this type of training is capturing. You will have to learn to be very observant with your dogs and capture desirable behavior en masse or individually. This will become second nature in time. As often as possible, you will ignore bad behavior that is not dangerous and instead, you will redirect the offender to the behavior that you would prefer. With time, positive training will become simpler and more intuitive.

Capturing the behavior refers to catching your dog doing what you want him to do and marking it the moment with the aforementioned marker word or clicker.

Requiring a "sit" for every important resource that you provide to your dogs is a good start to establishing your role of the benevolent leader. Do this with no exceptions — at least at first — and you will have built the first level of your foundation for a smoothly running multiple dog household. Requiring a "sit" helps you establish a pattern of manners, and it gives your dogs a default behavior to offer you. If you ask for or expect a "sit" many times throughout your normal daily routine, your dog will know that this makes you happy. Win/win for everyone.

> Trading manners from your dog for resources from you gives your dog a job to do. It also gives him the opportunity to play a part in a successful outcome from the behavior that he chooses to exhibit. Having the knowledge of the behavior that is expected of him creates a happier and more confident dog.

A word about asking for a "sit", though; again, know the basics of positive reinforcement and especially, capturing. Repeating the word "sit" over and over again will not establish a good pattern. It will just make you sound like a broken record. Learn how to capture the good behaviors, whether those good behaviors are a "sit" or other behaviors you want to increase. You also need to learn how to properly acknowledge your dogs' offerings. Remember that in general, no one works for free; show your dogs you appreciate their efforts. Another important term you should learn in order to train is luring. Being familiar with these will help you enormously. Learn the difference between a lure and a bribe and a reward. For a more complete explanation on capturing, rewards and lures, see Proofing the Pups.

As I began writing this book, I asked various people what they wanted to read about regarding multiple dogs. My friend Sue wondered whether quiet was ever possible. Well, sure it is. Again, that whole benevolent leadership thing goes a long way towards accomplishing this goal. But some chaos is part of the fun of having multiple

> A lure is a visible treat that you use to shape your dog into doing a behavior that he is just learning. A reward is a treat (or other valued prize) that you offer after your dog has completed said behavior. A bribe is an improperly used lure and/or reward.

TRENT, MERLIN AND KERA HAPPILY ENJOYING A FALL DAY EXERCISING OFF LEASH.

dogs! So allow some chaos once your benevolent leadership role is fully established, just not in the house too often unless you have an area set aside specifically for dog play. Playing is important to your dogs. All work and no play makes Fluffy a bored pup! See the chapter Play by Play for more info on play. But do set limits where and when you want calm. I strongly believe in permitting my dogs to go anywhere in my home (except the yucky basement!) but I do require manners in most every circumstance, even during play. And I do strive for calmness in the house most of the time.

Regular Exercise Makes For A Happier Crew

One thing you can easily do on a daily basis to help your dogs be calmer is to provide opportunities for an appropriate amount of exercise. I imagine that there is a wide divergence among readers regarding exercise: some of you personally get exercise on a regular basis and some of you don't. Those who do exercise know how far this practice can go towards helping to relieve stress. It's the same for your dogs. Exercise relieves frustration and it helps calm anxiety and stress. It also gives your dogs a much-needed change of scenery. Think about it: you very likely go places on a daily basis, and have the opportunity to see new sights. Your dogs do not have the option of choosing to do so themselves. They are dependent on you for this. So if you don't choose to exercise them on a regular basis outside of the home/yard, then they have the same-old, same-old. How long could you go with the same-old, same-old? Think cabin fever and maybe you grasp what I am getting at here.

All those sights and especially the smells that exist outside of your home are environmental stimuli that can help your dog to be mentally tired. Add that to the physical exercise that a walk, run or hike can give and you have a tired and relaxed dog. Even short walks are helpful because of the smells; a dog gets a wonderfully enriching experience just by sniffing the scents along the path. But the exercise is important as well. Giving your dogs exercise away from your own property on a daily basis is one of the best things you can do for them.

So you have a large fenced yard and your dogs play together a lot on a regular basis. You play ball or other physical games with your dogs as well. Do you think this is plenty of exercise? Well, it definitely contributes to your dogs' overall exercise allotment, but it certainly doesn't eliminate the need for walks away from your property. Again, say yes to environmental stimuli and no to cabin fever. Getting your crew outside to smell the pee smells is half the battle. A tired dog, both physically and mentally, is a calm dog. Exercise is a valuable tool in the multiple dog household!

> Making a decision to give your dogs regular outdoor exercise is a decision that you will never regret. They will thank you for it with a calmer demeanor.

Calming Accessories are Your Friend

Establishing a calm environment is a priority, and so I'd like to tell you about some wonderful calming products that can make your life with multiple dogs so much easier. Believe it or not, a wide selection of products can assist you greatly in achieving calm in the house and even outside of it. One of the handiest is a product called D.A.P. Comfort Zone®. This product approximates the pheromone that a dog's mother secretes to calm her young. Use the spray version of this product and spray it liberally on the soft surfaces in any room where you need calm. D.A.P.® also makes a plug-in version that is best used in small-to-medium sized rooms, not big open spaces. Another great product that I use on a daily basis is Aromadog Chill Out spray. This aromatherapy product calms both people and dogs.

I keep one on each floor of my home and one in my training bag. Shake it up for a few seconds and spray it liberally around any room. You can also spray it in a cloud around the dogs, taking care not to spray them directly in the face, of course! Please do heed the couple of exceptions for use (dogs prone to asthma and/or seizures). I spray this in the doorway before we leave to go to the park and I also spray my bedroom with it before I leave the house, as this is where my dogs usually hang out when I am gone. Another favorite product is Bach Rescue Remedy®. Bach produces a variety of flower essences, and this formulation is especially useful to calm your more anxious or rambunctious dogs. It is safe to use several times daily. It typically takes approximately fifteen minutes to be at full strength so keep that in mind if you are using it for a particular event. It lasts about two hours on average. You can also put it directly in your dog's water on a regular basis. For most uses, put two to four drops or sprays directly into your dog's mouth. If directly administering the remedy will cause anxiety, you can also put it on your hand and rub it on your dog's gums and/or belly.

Before you dive into the other sections, you may be interested in how I got to this point: life with multiple dogs.

My Story: When One, Two or Even Three is Not Enough

My love affair with dogs started later than some dog lovers' do. I was twenty years old and had just moved to southern Georgia with my then-husband. Our very good friends made the mistake of getting an eight week old puppy with an infant in the house. It made for chaos. Enter Debby and hubby. I had never had a dog before. When I was growing up, we lived in an apartment, and no dogs were allowed. I had cats and hamsters and even cared for a horse but no dogs. Well, I happily took that puppy in as my own. That puppy – Samantha, a perky twenty-five pound Pekingese/Chihuahua mix, was the beginning of a new life for me. I had always thought of myself as primarily a cat person but I loved all animals. My marriage didn't last, but my love affair with dogs is still going strong.

Samantha lived until the age of eleven and might have lived longer had her epilepsy medication not ruined her liver. Three weeks after Samantha's loss left me crushed and crying in bed whenever I was not at work, a neighbor's daughter knocked at my door carrying a large (fifty lb.) Shepherd mix in her arms. She had seen this very scared dog running loose near her school and smuggled the dog home on the school bus. Her mother had given her an ultimatum: get rid of the dog or she would take her to the shelter. The daughter knew that I had just lost my Samantha and thought that I might want her.

The last thing I wanted at that time was a replacement. I had lost my world. I only wanted Samantha back. But I didn't want anything to happen to this pretty dog and I agreed to keep her until her owners claimed her. Three weeks went by and the dog was still with me. I didn't even like big dogs. Even if I would get another dog, I told myself, I wanted another little dog. I prayed and prayed even though Layla, as I had named her, was easily the most serene and laid back dog I had ever met. She never chewed anything inappropriate, she was perfectly house trained and she was very polite about everything.

Finally, a phone call came from a couple of young kids who saw my ad in the Pennysaver, who claimed they owned her. Their description matched what I knew; they even knew about the rope leash she had been dragging, information I had purposely left out of the ad. And when I called the dog by the name they gave her - "Cindy" - she looked scared. I told them to have their mother contact me and we could talk about a return, but I was uneasy about the things they told me about the life they led. I guess I had the answer to my prayers because they never called back and I knew that Layla was mine. So much for little dogs! I was thrilled.

Layla and I had a great life together for five wonderful years, before I lost her to complications from seizures. When Layla was alive, I tried to add another canine playmate to our happy household but Layla wanted me to herself. So we stayed a single dog home until she crossed the rainbow bridge.

Three weeks after that loss, I was spending every spare moment walking dogs at the local shelter. It was my first week walking the "upstairs" dogs — dogs who were either new or sick. There was a lanky three month old black and tan ball of curly fur. The staff began calling him Figaro because of his curly black coat. I knew that I did not want a puppy so his allure was wasted on me at first. During our walk, Figaro gave me knowing looks with eyes that seemed far wiser than his years or even his species. Surely, I was imagining that depth of intelligence? I had to remind myself and him, "I do not want a puppy! I don't want to housetrain!" Again, he grinned and looked sideways at me. He then promptly stopped and did his business on the walk, showing me that he didn't need any stinking housetraining, thank you very much! He grinned at me again and seemed to say "so what do ya think now?" I sighed and my fight was lost right then and there. I returned to the shelter and said that I wanted to adopt him and would get him the following weekend after I got all the things I would need for a puppy. I renamed him Merlin, and this dog – my first boy dog - became my soul dog. He taught me many lessons, especially that trust must go both ways.

I was determined to be a two dog owner, so I often scoped the available dogs at the shelter, looking for a proper companion for my baby boy. About two months later, as we were arriving to pick up a blonde Shepherd mix named Gypsy for an overnighter, a fellow volunteer popped out the back door of the shelter with a stunningly beautiful all white puppy that appeared to be a Shepherd mix. Merlin play bowed to her and she galloped happily right back. I was later told that was her first animation since arriving at the shelter. She had been part of a "collector rescue" and had not had much in the way of human contact. Sadly, that happens when an animal lover goes too far and loses the ability to say no to dogs in need.

Merlin and I took Gypsy, the blonde Shepherd, home and it was a disaster. She hated Merlin's puppy playfulness and anytime he tried to play with her, she tried to hurt him. Back she went the next morning, sadly. We went straight to the adoption desk and asked about the beautiful white puppy who had play bowed to Merlin. I was told that there were already two applications ahead of mine and being a volunteer would not help me jump ahead. Merlin and I were nervously waiting – we had to get her, it was meant to be! Days went by and finally the phone call came in. The other applicants had never followed up and Daisy, as she was known at the time, was ours! Hurrah!

We arrived to get her and Merlin looked as pleased with himself as he could get. He appeared to think that I was buying him the best toy of all. They frolicked in the lobby and he led her to the car. I packed her in the backseat and Merlin climbed in the front. About half way home, his expression changed. He seemed to realize that he was now going to share me with Kera (formerly Daisy); even if he wanted this new "toy", sharing was not something that Merlin appeared to desire. So he alternated between loving and playing happily with Kera, and play fighting with her to "show her who was boss". Of course, I permitted no rough stuff, but that did not stop my first boy dog from trying. Within a week, however, they were fast friends, sleeping in exactly the same position next to each other, playing side by side, eating politely next to each other, sharing everything. I could not have been happier! I felt that I had all that I would ever need with these two dogs. Little did I know it would not stop there!

Through Merlin's ancestry, I was introduced to the world of Doberman Pinschers. I was enchanted by my first boy dog. I had to know everything about this breed that he resembled. I met people on the internet who introduced me to the rescue world, and soon I was joining them. Within months, we took in Lady, my first Doberman foster dog. What fun! We were three!

Merlin has so much energy; there were never enough dogs to play with. All he wanted to do was play. And his temperament was so wonderful. He never reacted to any show of aggression from another dog. He displayed all the right body language to let them know he meant no harm. He just wanted to play, that's all. I was in love! Kera didn't like Lady very much, so over the course of a year, my new friend in central PA and I shared custody of her, trying to find Lady the perfect home and working on behavioral issues. Finally we had success! Months and then years went by and we took in foster dog after foster dog, all successfully re-homed. My love of dogs was becoming a full-time enterprise as I plunged deep into the world of breed rescue.

When Merlin and Kera were three years old, I responded to a post on an internet list from someone asking for help with a serious rescue situation. Her co-worker, whose female Rottweiler had puppies by the neighbor's German Shepherd, was threatening to drown the puppies once they reached a certain age! To make matters worse, these puppies had to leave their mother much too early, and at four weeks were kept in a medical foster home until they were healthy. Because there were seven of them. they were nicknamed the seven Dwarves. Two of the boys —Bashful and Grumpy—ended up staying at that foster home (renamed Alexander and Amadeus), and the other five came to my house. A female (Happy) found a home right away, so the remaining four—Dopey, Sleepy, Sneezy & Doc, two boys and two girls—stayed with me. They were tiny and adorable, to start with anyway. As weeks passed, they grew larger and heavier.

Another friend became an adopter and claimed a boy and a girl together, renaming those two, Maximus and Niko. Soon, someone came to see the remaining two and decided on the last boy, aptly named Dopey and renamed him Debo. That left one girl, who was now eleven weeks old. My Kera, who had hated these puppies throughout their stay, suddenly decided that she liked this girl, Sleepy. I decided the name had to go and did some research, renaming her Siri, a shortened feminine version of Sirius, the Dog Star. As Kera showed more and more affection for Siri, we decided to keep her. Merlin loved all of the puppies from day one, so having his very own puppy to play with was like a dream come true to him. He would lie on the floor and let them all run all over him. He loved to grumble at them and gently show them who was boss. Now he had a little girl who adored him on a regular basis. What more could a boy ask for?? So then there were three.

After that, I again went back to fostering Dobermans on a regular basis. I usually had at least four dogs in my home at all times. One Doberman in particular made a huge impression on me and his name was Damon. It turned out that Damon had a disease well known in the breed known as Wobbler's Syndrome or Cervical Instability; CVI for short. I decided to keep Damon and found a fund that would assist with his care, which was very expensive, indeed. Damon did live longer than my regular vet predicted, but his spine just wasn't well and I had to let him go about eight months later.

I was very happy when I had four dogs of my own. But part of my happiness at having multiple dogs is being able to fully manage the needs of each dog. Not all of my dogs needed to go on long walks, so that enabled me to give each dog what he or she needed. That is something that I feel is very important if you are going to make a commitment to having multiple dogs for the long run. It's less stressful on everyone if not all need more than is easy to give.

But sometimes fate intervenes with happiness, as with Damon. After Damon's loss, I decided to leave the rescue group that gave me my start and organize my own, sticking within my own geographic area. It was becoming too hard to go back and forth between Pittsburgh and Harrisburg and I wanted a break. The volunteers that were in my area remained with me and we named the new group, Damon's Den Doberman Rescue of Western PA, in memory of Damon. I continued to have Doberman fosters dogs and many passed through my home on their way to new and better existences. Most we helped, but there were a couple that were too badly damaged. It would have been a bad idea to place them so I held them as they passed over the Rainbow Bridge. That never gets easier, I am afraid.

One day while working at a day job, my then boss asked me if I could help her son place his Pitbull mix and I referred her someone I knew who did all breed rescue, specializing in Pitbulls. She turned out to be a collector rather than a rescuer. Humane agents discovered the sad truth and I felt it was my duty to take him into my rescue and place him responsibly myself. That was over four years ago and now, Trent is mine. He is still a work in progress but he has come far and he is a very loving dog. Onward we persevere! So now I have four dogs that do require a lot of exercise and I still foster dogs for my rescue group. It has been a lot of work but it has been extremely rewarding and I would not have it any other way. It gets me exercised frequently as well. If this hasn't scared you into shutting the book, then let's carry on and meet the real life scenario contributors.

JOY AND DOUG FROM GIBSONIA, *PA have eight dogs total; three large and five small. Brody, Rhett and Brandy are Dobermans. Aries, Sierra, Joe and Gunnar are Min Pins. Dan is a Jack Russell Terrier.*

JEN AND JEFF, CURRENTLY LIVING IN WV, *have four dogs at present. Takoda is a Doberman mix, Oskar is a Rottweiler/Lab mix, Ruby (foster dog) is a Min Pin and Jasmine is a Doberman.*

CHERI & RUSS IN BUTLER, *PA currently have three dogs. Delanie, Socretes and Gizmo are all Border Collies. They have had up to seven dogs at once in the past, all but one Border Collies.*

SUE AND LAURA FROM PITTSBURGH, *PA have three dogs at present. Amadeus (Deus) and Alexander (Xander) are the brothers of my* dog, Siri. They also have a tiny little girl named Ana, who is a Chihuaha mix. Before Ana joined them, they had Mona, their dearly beloved White Shepherd mix.

CRYSTAL AND ROSS FROM INDIANA, PA have five dogs at this time. Sally is a Border Collie/Retriever mix; Sammy, George and Dover are all English Setters; Toby is an Irish Setter.

JOYCE AND ALAN OF HEIDELBERG, PA have three dogs. Jessie is a Great Dane/Lab mix, Kendra is a Rottweiler/Doberman mix and Baxter is a Border Collie mix.

CHRIS AND MICHAEL IN WASHINGTON STATE have three dogs. Paris is a ten year old Lab, Cherokee is an adolescent German Shepherd Dog. Apache is a German Shepherd Dog puppy.

LILIAN FROM PITTSBURGH, PA is also a professional dog trainer. She has three dogs of her own at this time. JJ is a Collie mix, Phoenix is a Greyhound and Titan is a Collie/Jack Russell Terrier mix. She also often has foster dogs in her home.

SUSAN FROM PITTSBURGH, PA has three dogs. Chelsea is a Border Collie, and Candy and Crystal are both Australian Shepherds

Chapter 2

Doggone Relax Already!
Carving Calm Out of Chaos

Now we will address calming particulars in several important locations in your home.

Kitchen Relaxation

So what do you do when you're trying to prepare dinner and dogs are underfoot? Let's talk about how to hang out in the kitchen when you have guests and food is abundant. (For tips on how to handle your dogs' mealtime manners, read the Mealtime Manners chapter) When you (and your guests) are in the kitchen, your dogs should be calm. They can be interested in what is going on and what is being prepared but they should not be too interested. Don't tolerate dogs sticking their noses in too close to bowls and stoves and such. My dogs lie around the kitchen while I prepare meals and they are fine in the kitchen when we have guests. I can trust them not to take food off of tables and counters. They are more interested in some meal prep than others but nosing in is not acceptable behavior, and I redirect them to another area and use a down cue if they get too nosy. Getting in my way in the kitchen while I am trying to work is a personal pet peeve of mine. This is the behavior that I address first in my own kitchen with any new dog.

Be aware that teaching manners in this room in particular will be

> Teaching your dogs to disregard food items that you have not given them will be one of the harder things you will teach, but if you teach this behavior at a slow and steady pace, you will be rewarded with solid success!

probably more challenging than other rooms in your home. It's hard to be good with all that food around, right? To our dogs, we are the best hunters ever! And then we cook it too. It doesn't get much better! So this is where you will use many cues that you have taught your dogs. Many cues come to mind: "sit", "down", "leave it", "drop it", "off".

> Tethering, quite simply, means that you leash your dog to something. Preferably something sturdy if you have a large dog. This is a handy way to limit his area when need be. This is something that should only be done when supervised.

If some or all of your dogs are not ready for all of these cues and they require too much supervision in the kitchen, then consider tethering those that need it. This is only meant to be used when you are in the room to supervise. It is also best done with a chain leash, especially if there is a chance that your dog might quickly chew a fabric or leather leash. Tethering can teach your dog to relax while taking away some of the freedom that would get him into trouble. This will give you an opportunity to reward the tethered dog for appropriate behavior. Giving a tethered dog something to occupy himself with while tethered is a good idea. Of course, that requires every dog getting some reward whether tethered or not. You might have a dog or two that has no need of tethering. Great! Make sure that you reward that good behavior well. Make it clear how happy this makes you. You will also be rewarding the tethered dog(s) for every calm moment. As far as what you should be tethering dogs to in your kitchen, well, I will leave that to your own common sense. If you have large dogs, the heavier the item the better!

Make sure that you choose something sturdy that does not permit them to reach you or any tempting food. One behavior that you might want to integrate into this tethering situation is a "go to mat" behavior. This is a portable safe and calm place that will be that dog's spot. Refer to Proofing the Pups for help teaching this behavior. You can easily use a towel for each dog or buy them each a flat dog bed for just this purpose. While you tether a dog, also give them their mat to lie on and they will each learn that this is their spot. Give un-tethered dogs a mat as well.

The important thing to remember when choosing a mat is that it be more flat than fluffy. Fluffy is too bed-like. You are not looking for another dog bed. You are looking for a visual marker with a mat. A mat is a very clearly seen space that belongs to your dog.

So even if you have a dog or two that does not need to be tethered, the mat will establish that they have a spot to be calm. This also helps each dog to improve focus. You will need to be aware of each dog's level of calmness to evaluate when that dog should graduate to the next level of freedom. You want your dogs to learn to be calm without tethering. You also need not graduate all dogs at the same time. This is another part of the "life is not fair" theory. Base your decision to remove a tether on the behavior of the individual, not a group.

Capture and reward desirable behavior. I cannot repeat this too much! Be calm when you reward for calm but make it notable. It is best to set up times when you can train for this, ideally without a house full of visitors. You can start when you are simply hanging out in your kitchen doing something besides cooking, then progress to training when you are preparing meals. Make it a part of your routine and take it from there. Use your best judgment on graduating a dog, and if a dog slips up and finds something too tempting, then simply re-tether. That works sort of like a time out. Think positive and you will get positive. Expect the best. Expect calm. I am a big believer in the power of positive thinking. Try it!

Compliance problems, in a nutshell, mean that a dog is not doing what was asked of him. This can include growling or snapping when asked to get off furniture, or guarding a favorite spot from a human or another dog. Compliance problems can be multi-faceted. A serious compliance problem involving furniture should be a reason to keep a dog from sharing any furniture with you.

Living/Family Room Relaxation

Whether you permit your dogs on your furniture or not is up to you. There is no right or wrong choice unless you are having some compliance problems with a dog or two; in that case, that dog should not be permitted to sit on furniture (or laps, if it is a small dog) for now. What is a compliance problem? I provide more details about compliance problems in *Let Sleeping Does Lie* but it's relevant here as well. If any of your dogs guard wherever they lie, especially when on raised surfaces, then they should not be allowed to lie there, period. Another compliance problem you may encounter in this room is a dog guarding a favorite human from the other dogs. Don't permit this either. If any type of guarding is going on, get professional assistance and do not permit a dog that behaves this way on raised surfaces. If none of these situations apply to you and your dogs, and if you want to snuggle on furniture with your dogs, then go for it. Hopefully, if that is the case, you have enough furniture for all of your dogs and your human family! If not, or even if so, there should be dog beds in sufficient supply that all of your dogs have a place to lie down and relax in this room.

Assuming that your is family is like most families, then you spend a great deal of downtime in this room. Since your dogs are part of your family, they need places and belongings to call their own. One of the problems that I encounter frequently in my private sessions with clients, is that some families forget that their dogs need their

COLLINS-JOHNSON CREW RELAXING IN THE LIVING ROOM.

own belongings, too. Many people expect their dogs to ignore everything in the home that is not theirs, yet they give them nothing of their own; toys and beds are limited to one room or special moments. This should not be the case. Your dogs are part of your family and a family member has basic needs. This includes having something of their own that they can turn to when they need comfort or recreation. So if you remedy this situation, you'll add another ingredient to the recipe for a calm and relaxing room.

A BED AND A TOY BOX IN THE LIVING ROOM.

Dog beds and toy boxes are two additions you won't regret. I have a toy box and dog beds in every room in my house except the bathroom and kitchen. I would add both to my kitchen if it was farther away from my living room, but the living room toy basket is convenient to both rooms. So to help your dogs to be more relaxed let them know that they are an integral part of the family by offering these for their use in the rooms that

Dog beds need not be pricey. If you are watching pennies, then use folded blankets to provide additional comfortable places for your dogs to lie. Thrift stores also offer great values as do dollar stores. Be creative!

are important to you. You will be amazed at the difference this small change makes. As far as dog beds go, if your dogs are permitted on furniture, then don't worry about matching the quantity of dogs to the quantity of beds; if not, then be aware of your dog's habits.

TRENT, SIRI, AND KERA RELAXING ON A DOG BED IN THE LIVING ROOM. EVERYONE SHARES AVAILABLE RELAXATION SPACE WELL.

Some dogs like simply lying on the carpet or cool uncarpeted floors. Some will be upset when this is the only option presented, and will likely leave the room for another, more comfortable room.

Make it clear to your dogs that you like having them nearby when you are relaxing. Verbally acknowledge them. If there are not enough dog beds, toss pillows on the floor. I have two dog beds in my living room but I also have a huge couch and a loveseat that my dogs are permitted on. I toss the huge decorative couch pillows on the floor to add another makeshift dog bed. When I have a foster dog, they relax in this room with the rest of the family. My foster dogs are permitted on the dog beds and the loveseat but not on the couch.

I will tether dogs in this room that need to be tethered, but I have only had to do that with one puppy in all the time I have been living with multiple dogs. Usually, the foster dogs stick to the loveseat or the dog beds. Of course, if your dogs are wound up and in need of exercise and/or something sturdy to chew on, you may have to tether a bit more frequently than I do! But this is where those toy boxes come in handy. Have a nice supply of interactive toys in this room such as various Kong® products, empty marrow bones, Premier Tug-a-Jugs™, etc.

SIRI AND HER BIG BALL.

You can also supply soft toys as well, as long as your dogs don't eat the insides. Most dogs are fine with soft toys and if you are around to supervise, then all should be well. A word about soft toys: shredding them is a perfectly normal behavior and they belong to your dogs, so don't chastise them for shredding them. If you don't want to pay big cash for toys that get shredded, just buy them at a Dollar Store or a thrift shop. I buy stuffed toys in large batches at a thrift shop and sort through them to remove anything inappropriate (bean stuffed toys, items that can easily be pulled off, etc.). Your dogs will love you for it. They can have great fun in a group picking them apart or just lying around squeaking them. Some dogs use stuffed toys as a sort of security. Siri, who is my largest dog, has a very large furry stuffed ball that is at least twice the size of her head; she carries that toy in her mouth everywhere she goes in the house.

If any of your dogs are guarding their toys, then you might need to consider tethering that dog until these issues are handled. DON'T take chances with high-value toys/treats until you feel confident the guarding behavior is gone, especially if you live alone. It's just not worth it. I know people who have multiple dogs who have simply

Guarding high value belongings from the other dogs can be a minor or a major issue. It is natural for a dog to not want to surrender a valued item to another dog. But it should not come to blows. And as the benevolent leader, you should be vigilant about preventing pushiness from either side.

found it easier to always tether their dogs in a relaxing family room situation when passing out high value chew options. If this solution works for you, that is fine; do be aware, however, that if something high-value falls into dog territory or if someone other than you or your immediately family hands out a treat to dogs who have a tendency to guard, a melee could occur. It's better to treat the issue slowly but surely and practice good management techniques until you accomplish this. Rest assured, it can be done!

A word on playing in the house: I do permit my dogs to play in my living room with some limits. I have large rooms and sturdy furniture. I also have very graceful dogs for the most part. They stick to the center of the room and wrestle appropriately. If the action gets out of hand, I interrupt it. Siri will also ask to go outside (by ringing the bell on the door) if she wants more room to wrestle. If the weather is appropriate, I will then let them outside to continue.

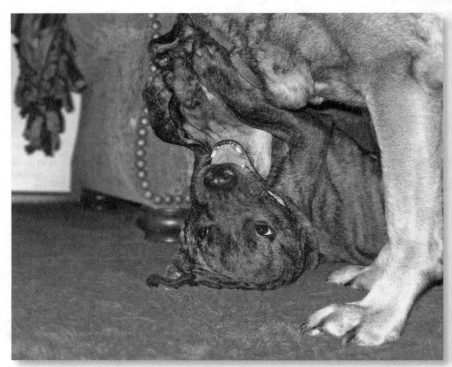

TRENT AND SIRI ENJOYING INDOOR PLAYTIME. AS LONG AS IT IS NOT DESTRUCTIVE, INDOOR PLAY IS HEALTHY FOR YOUR DOG.

You will have to decide whether a bit of playing in your living/family room is appropriate for you. It depends on your situation.

Bedroom Relaxation

Teaching your dogs to relax in the bedroom is very much like teaching them to relax in the living/family room, except the focus should be more on sleep than toys or chewies. Much depends, of course, on how you use your bedroom. If you tend to retire to your bedroom to watch TV before you intend to sleep, it's unreasonable to expect your dogs to immediately go to sleep when you won't be! So quiet chewing should be permissible, again keeping in mind any guarding issues. For a complete description of multiple dog bedroom etiquette, see *Let Sleeping Dogs Lie*. For now, let's assume that you have a safe and comfortable place for all dogs to sleep, whether that includes your bed or another family member's bed or just a comfy dog beds on the floor. Comfort in the sleeping quarters is of utmost importance, to humans and dogs alike. Humans and dogs like to feel safe, and while sleeping, everyone is vulnerable. If your dogs sleep on the floor on dog beds (a perfectly acceptable situation), make sure that these beds are not in the path that you take on your way to the bathroom in the middle of the night in the dark. It's not nice to be woken up by being stepped on. Some dogs are not especially friendly in that type of situation and you can hardly blame them. So consider safety when arranging a relaxing pattern for your dogs in your bedroom.

The bedroom is another great place for a handy toy box, should you have need of distractions here. Chewing on a bone or a favorite toy is very relaxing to a dog. Most dogs will automatically be more relaxed in the bedroom but if you have that

> Make sure there are enough safe and comfortable places for all of your dogs to spend their sleeping hours. Scatter beds in various places away from one another spots to avoid nighttime skirmishes if need be.

unusual dog who is wound up no matter where he is, then again consider tethering. Chewing is important in this case, perhaps even more so, as you will simply have a very frustrated dog on a leash if you offer him nothing to do. As far as crating goes, if you crate any of your dogs for sleeping, you can still offer chewing options here as well. Low key activity is the secret to calm in the bedroom. Many of the steps you would take to make your bedroom a calm respite for your own relaxation will work for the canines in your life.

SIRI, KERA AND TRENT HAVING DAYTIME RELAXATION IN THE BEDROOM.

If I am going to bed early with the intention of watching TV or reading before sleeping, my dogs can tell the difference. They tend to sprawl over the floor and maybe the dog beds. They dip into the "bone box" and grab something to chew. Merlin sometimes uses this time frame to dip into the toy box and "kill a bunny". That is my term for his once-a-month (or so) meticulous shredding of a stuffed toy, after tossing all of the stuffed toys all over the bedroom. It seems to be a release for him and I am okay with this. He does not race around the room; his behavior is pretty low key and it's a precursor to lying

> Provide low-key interactive toys in an easily accessible toy box. Do not permit roughhousing in the bedroom in the evening. Consider tethering an unruly dog when needed.

down to sleep for him. It also seems to amuse the other dogs. The key here is to know your dogs. Know what riles them up and what helps them relax and act and react accordingly. Your instincts will serve you well here. I do not ever permit playing in this room at night. I do allow my dogs to play in here during the day, however;

they can tell the difference between bedtime and daytime. Dogs are smarter than we often give them credit for. There are, of course, several books to support this. See the reference section for these selections.

Doorway/Entry Way Relaxation

While your doorway is not a hangout spot, this is an area of your home where your dog should learn to relax. But be aware that relaxation at the entry way to your home does not come without hard work in many cases. For specific details on training specific cues that can assist you with this and other issues, see Proofing the Pups. Multiple dogs are harder to train for doorway calmness than a single dog is so there will be several options offered here. I won't lie and say my dogs are the best at this situation. They are loud and intimidating if they don't know you. I have not bothered to train this for strangers because simply put, I don't get many visitors that either my dogs or I don't know or that are not dog people (we all stick together) so it doesn't matter to me.

When I do have "normal" people visitors (and it's usually rescue-related such as someone coming to adopt my foster dog), then I use a baby gate to keep the dogs in the next room. This way, the dogs can see the visitors and know what is going on but they don't get to come in. One of my dogs is a barker in this situation but it is important to me that he is mostly aware of what is transpiring (again, rescue-related) so I do use calming accessories in this situation as well. If he still insists on barking, a "time out" where he has to go into the yard alone usually does it as he really wants to be central to the action. He doesn't want to risk banishment after the first time.

Regarding service people and others who are only going to be at your home on a very irregular basis: it's simply not worth the effort to integrate your dogs with them. Just put the dogs in a different area of the house. Unless of course, they are perfectly behaved! But if they are anything less than this, just give them all something wonderful to occupy themselves with and let the service person do his job. If you allow them the opportunity to act inappropriately on a regular basis, this effectively rewards their

> Give your dogs something yummy to chew on and place them into another room when service people visit.

inappropriate behavior and the bad behavior will not go away. Reward them for their appropriate behavior when the service person is gone and let them sniff around. Service person visits don't need to be traumatic.

If you have relatives or friends over periodically whom your dogs know but are not completely familiar with so much that they are immediately comfortable, then these are people who you might possibly want to try and get your dogs more comfortable with. It's best to wait on the dog greetings until you get your visitor into the house itself. Doorways are actually one of the places that are most exciting to dogs. This includes all doorways partially because they are narrow in comparison to a room, but also because they contain the element of surprise. Entry ways are the most exciting of all doorways. Having your dogs greet visitors inside of the house away from the door is better for everyone. You might try letting only one or two of your dogs meet these people first. Then add one at a time. Either use baby gates or other rooms to separate dogs until you want them added to the mix.

> Have your dogs greet visitors one at a time until they are fully trained as a group. It reduces the greeting energy. Use baby gates or closed doors as needed. Have the greetings away from the actual entry way to your home in a calmer area.

The group greeting is far more energetic. Dogs feed on group energy much like people do. If you make the greeting procedure more personal and one on one, you will have created more of a calming zone. Choose the calmest dog(s) to be in the welcoming committee. The rest will likely be barking, wherever you have chosen to confine them, but be firm and absolutely do not give any others entry to the greeting room until they have quieted down. Depending on how many dogs you have, add only one at a time or two at most.

If you have any dogs who are potentially dangerous when meeting people in your home, then you should certainly get help from a professional trainer. Obviously, if you have such a dog, then don't place anyone in danger. But keep in mind that if you always avoid letting the dog meet people, you will never give him a chance to improve his behavior.

Another option is to bring the dogs outside to meet the visitors.

This can help fearful dogs feel a bit more comfortable. However, it can be a handful to bring all of your dogs outside in order to greet people before they enter your home. If only a few of your dogs have issues with overly-excited in-home greetings, this may be easier for you to man-

> An alternate behavior can really be helpful to reduce high energy greetings. It is especially comforting to fearful dogs.

age—providing, of course, that your guests don't mind this proce-dure! When deciding if this might be effective for you, keep in mind how your dogs behave when they are on leash and meet strangers. If their behavior in this situation is worse than their indoor greeting behavior, this is not the option for you. My own dogs are primarily guarding breeds so when they are on leash, particularly as a large group, they greet strangers who try and approach us close up in a suspicious manner. That is basically what I have taught them to do. We live in the city and that is behavior I want. However, after the ini-tial burst of alert barking at visitors to my home, known or unknown, they are pretty friendly with invited visitors so inside is better for me. The key here is to know your dogs.

Other things that you can do to improve door greetings without banishing them to other areas of the home include teaching them an alternate behavior for when they hear a knock or a doorbell. For instance, teach them to go somewhere other than the door: a crate, a mat or even a separate room can all be used for this. Step-by-step instructions for most alternate behaviors will not be included here, but the "go to mat" instructions are included in the training section. My instructions do not include using a doorbell or a knock as a cue for going to the mat but you can easily add that in once you have progressed in teaching it. What "go to mat" basically entails is teaching your dogs to go to a specified place when they hear the knock or the doorbell. That will be their cue. You can use either a crate or a separate room to teach the same thing. Just modify the step-by-step instructions for that use.

If you decide to use a crate, realize that you will need to have one at the ready for each dog at all times. This is why I prefer a mat or even a different room. You will have to teach this with your dogs one at a time, then as a group, as in all the training recommendations. And realize that this will not happen overnight. So be patient! You will need assistance for doorbell ringing/knocking. Just as with a

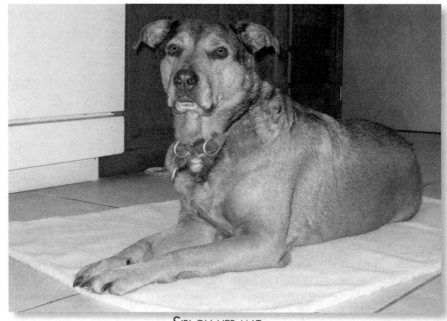

SIRI ON HER MAT.

crate, the mat must be available to each dog at all times or teaching the behavior won't help. But a mat is unobtrusive and can be placed anywhere. You can also just use them when you are actually just expecting company and simply take your chances with unexpected knocks/rings. But this behavior will certainly go far more smoothly if each dog can always locate a mat. So be prepared if you prefer calm. Mats are handy things to have and teach a dog to go to. This behavior can be used in multiple situations. The mat will be considered a safe place for your dogs to go to in any situation that one is available to them. Siri loves her mat. It helps her to relax and feel safe anywhere that I take her, even if there is a roomful of people there.

Yard and Porch Relaxation

If your dogs are regular yard terrorists; policing the fence line, blasting the perimeter, barking at anything and everything, then the only way to even begin to address this is to always supervise when they are out. The less they are permitted to practice this behavior, the better the chances that you can train them to relax in one of the most exciting of all places.

> Supervise, supervise, supervise when you have a dog who is reactive outdoors. It will give you the opportunity to be completely consistent until you can modify the behavior to your liking.

If you do not have a fenced yard, then obviously, your dogs should be leashed in the yard if they are not perfectly behaved, especially if you live in an urban or suburban environment. But even if they are perfectly behaved, a good amount of supervision is important when you have multiple dogs. The dogs will be more excitable when all together than they would be with only one or even two dogs. Spending time with your dogs when you are home is important to building and keeping a relationship that focuses on the partnership between you. When you are outside with your dogs, you should practice using your happiest voice to get them to check in with you. This increases the chance that they will come to you when you need them to. Excellent recalls are really important if you have no fencing and a decent amount of property. Do keep in mind that living in a more rural area is still not a license to permit your dogs to roam. It shortens their life span.

Even if you have fencing, I still recommend supervision if your dogs are not relaxed in the yard. If you are in the stage of choosing fencing, then choose privacy fencing—the taller the better. This takes away the fence fighting opportunity that often occurs with

NICOLAI, NIKKO AND STARBUCK RELAXING IN THE YARD USING TIE OUTS.

> Be ready to reward lavishly when your dogs check in with you when outside. Always reward away from the fence line for fence reactors. Keep sturdy toys available outside for distraction assistance.

see-through fences. If you have close neighbors with fences and dogs of their own (or dogs and no fences!) then you know what I mean. Such a situation is ripe for reactivity and supervision is necessary at all times. However, with privacy fencing, that need is much reduced and yard time will be much calmer overall. Privacy fencing is your friend. If the possibility of replacing fencing is out of the question and you need a calmer crew in the yard, then you have some work to do.

If your dogs are highly reactive when out in the yard, then teaching calm yard behavior is particularly important. It is also not something that can be safely and completely covered here, but I will give you some tips. The relationship building exercises come in very handy here and will help your dogs to learn to focus on you. The more fun that you make it to be closer to you, then the more your dogs will respond to you, even in the yard. Never ever give attention to your dogs at the fence line if they fence fight or charge the fence for any reasons. All rewards come when they are away from the fence. If you use a clicker, sitting in the yard and clicking/treating your dogs simply for coming to you, even if not asked, is a great way to train without actually doing anything active.

It will take time and obviously, the rewards MUST be high-value or the incentive will not be there. Squirrels, other dogs, cats, bicyclists, joggers, etc. will all undermine your efforts if your rewards don't rock. Yard toys are a handy thing to have. Think indestructible like Kongs®, Nylabones®, marrow bones, etc. A selection of balls will please many dogs, especially if you throw them. Remember, a tired dog is a calm dog. If you keep your dogs busy in the yard, they are focused on you and not outside influences.

> Untrained (and even many trained) dogs should be leashed in unfenced yards for safety. Supervise tethered dogs for safety.

Some dogs like to lie outside in their yards and relax. This is a good thing if you have the appropriate setting for this and again, if they are calm. Make sure that your area is safe to have unsupervised dogs in the yard. Of course, you could always hang out outside and relax with them. But remember, unsupervised dogs outside in an unprotected area can be in danger. If your dogs are outside in an unfenced yard unsupervised, also be aware of whether people walking by might perceive them as scary. Even if they are not doing anything wrong, some breeds or mixes of such breeds are scary to people and a scary looking dog in an unfenced yard is a recipe for a problem.

Should you tether outside? I believe that you should only tether your dog(s) outside if you are supervising frequently; tethers can come loose. They also increase reactivity and even create it by causing frustration. A tether traps your dog in one spot. If your dogs are not calm when in the yard then tethering is not for you at all.

What about trolley systems? It's not terribly practical for multiple dogs. They are another recipe for disaster, especially with breeds who chase things. Using a trolley system can increase reactivity and doesn't give you a calm dog in the yard. They are also not terribly safe. Sadly, I know of dogs who have strangled themselves on these systems.

What if you like to tether on your porch rather than in your yard? What if your porch is mostly or completely fenced and your dog respects that barriers? Many dogs like to pass some time watching the scenery from the porch but many others are as reactive in this situation as they are in a yard. Well, the same rules apply to porches that apply to yards. Also, keep in mind when and where your mail is delivered when deciding whether to tether your dogs on your porch. Mail carriers are not required to deliver mail where they feel threatened. It would benefit no one to scare the mail carrier and get your dog(s) maced! Be wise about permitting your dogs to be on your porch unsupervised. Know your dogs and know your neighborhood!

That brings us to electronic fencing systems. Let me state right off the bat that I am not a fan of these at all. There are so many cons. Rather than solving a confinement problem, they can create behavior problems in some dogs. Fence line running with these can

> Just say no to containment methods that may create pain, fear and/or danger. This includes electronic containment systems and overhead trolleys.

be even worse than with a barrier fence because the shock element is present. The training provided by the companies who sell and install these is rarely taught by someone with dog behavior knowledge. I could go on and on about why I don't like them. But I must be completely honest. I *have* seen them used responsibly. Some people cover the shock prongs on the collar and train the dog to respond to the warning tone only, which is a great idea. Others use them for specific purposes only, such as only at the front door opening onto a busy street, because they have young children in the house who open doors when they shouldn't. Or they have people in and out of their house a lot. Another former client of mine has far too many acres (eighty!) to fence with barrier fencing and her dogs have the run of about forty acres on electronic fencing. They have never hit the fence line. It works here, but keep in mind that situations like these are the exception rather than the rule. I get calls from dog owners all the time to help fix behavior problems that were caused by electronic fencing.

So you are contemplating a doggy door and you are wondering whether this will help your dogs or harm them? Well, if you have a safe privacy-fenced yard in a safe and calm neighborhood and your dogs are not prone to behave inappropriately when they hang out in the yard, then you may have a good idea here. If you have anything less than this, then think long and hard about installing a doggy door. Allowing multiple dogs unlimited access

> Know your neighborhood before giving your dogs full time access to your yard with a doggy door.

to your yard when you are not home can create a situation ripe for problems. Installing a doggy door that you could lock when you are not home may solve the problem. Think carefully about your dogs behavior and your neighborhood situation before you decide.

All in all, until your dogs are reliably calm in your yard, whatever your setup may be, it's best to supervise. Consistently rewarding only calm behavior in the yard will help you get your point across. Success comes with repetition. Repetition is your friend.

Hopefully you can use these suggestions to begin creating a calm home for your family members, human and canine.

Chapter 3

Mealtime Manners
Dining Without Incident

Feeding time in the multiple dog household can be chaotic or it can be calm. It is actually all based on how you approach it. I feed all of my own dogs together. When I have a foster dog in the house, I feed the foster dog separately. I have also fed said foster dogs in the same room as my dogs in the past. As long as your method works in your household, to each his own. I do generally recommend separating them though…more on that later. But there are important guidelines to follow whenever you are feeding two or more dogs at the same time.

If you are feeding everyone together, it is very important that you do not permit any posturing and stealing of another dog's food. Be on the lookout for any kind of guarding behavior. You will be glad that you have spent time teaching a reliable "leave it" cue in this scenario. The "leave it" behavior needs to be taught to each dog in your home individually and then proofed together as a group, as with every cue that you teach them. Further instructions for teaching "leave it" are available in Proofing the Pups.

> Posturing refers to a dog using his body language to try and intimidate another dog. This can include standing in a leaning position over another dog while they are trying to eat.

Remember what I said earlier about all good things coming from you? This is when it makes the most difference. If your dogs totally grasp that everything they get comes directly from you, there is much less of a chance that they will attempt to both-

> Proofing a behavior means that you are making it reliable in many circumstances.

THE DOG ON THE RIGHT IS TRYING TO INTIMIDATE THE DOG ON THE LEFT. THIS IS ONE OF MANY POSTURES THAT A DOG CAN USE TO TRY AND GET ANOTHER DOG TO MOVE AWAY FROM HIS FOOD. DO NOT PERMIT INTIMIDATION, ESPECIALLY DURING MEALTIMES.

er each other when food is involved. Dogs that are comfortable with your role as the benevolent leader will usually not have a problem eating in proximity to one another. Provide abundance for your dogs in their daily life on a regular basis and they will behave appropriately at mealtimes as well as in other high resource arenas.

Each dog should feel safe to eat his food without a disturbance. Of course, your dogs should be encouraged to eat in a timely manner, as you do not want to play the food police all morning and evening. I allow approximately half an hour or so for mealtime ingestion. This time frame is subject to change when I have places to go and people to see. At those times, I try to serve what I consider to be food that is faster to eat or is more enticing. But all in all, I try very hard to allow enough time for everyone to eat their meal in relatively leisurely peace.

> Be sure to provide enough space around each dog so that each can feel comfortable eating.

Trixie (foster dog), George, Dover, Sally and Toby maintaining a down stay prior to a meal, and then enjoying their meal.

In my house, each dog has his own space to eat, but there are no enclosures to prevent drifting. However, most of the time, they use what they have already learned: that it is improper to eye another dog's dinner if they finish first. I supervise the entire mealtime, occasionally running quickly into another room as needed. I have learned from experience that even the best-trained dog will sometimes try and use intimidation techniques to try to get a dog who is used to appeasing the others to hand over his dinner! It is my role as benevolent leader to discourage this, as the intimidating dog should not get another dog's dinner as reward. Hence, my reasoning for the

TRENT AND KERA HAVING BREAKFAST. THEIR BOWLS ARE FAR ENOUGH APART THAT EVERYONE FEELS SAFE EATING.

vigilant supervision. All it takes is a look from me if a dog is thinking of trying such a prank.

Most of the time, my dogs will eat when they are fed, but occasionally a dog or two is finicky. When Merlin was younger, he was very finicky. If you allow one dog to be finicky on a regular basis, believe me, they will continue to do what you are reinforcing. The key here is to find a middle ground between too fast and too slow. If you have a dog that eats meals more slowly than the others, make sure that you give him enough time to eat. But don't get into a habit of arranging your feeding schedule around him. You could be creating a chain of behavior where you have inadvertently rewarded him for not eating at mealtimes. In other words, the finicky dog will have learned that if he waits to eat, he will get special enticements and/or attention that the dogs who eat their dinner in a timely manner don't get. What has this dog taught you? That he is smarter than you! It is in your dog's best interests — and yours — to limit the time you leave the food down so that you can all get on with the other parts of your day.

> Don't cater to a finicky eater! He will simply get more finicky.

You will learn how long is too long with practice. So find that middle ground, but make sure that you do not rush your dog to eat. That is no better than allowing too much time and it's terrible for the digestion! On average, I leave the food down about as long as it takes me to eat my own meals plus the after-dinner cleanup. My dogs eat a raw diet so it will not be just a matter of my dogs immediately scarfing down their kibble. So do allow time for the type of meals you prepare for your crew. We have become a

> For more info on a raw diet and what it consists of, see the Resources section.

fast food society and look what it has done to us! It is in our best interests to eat normal meals and savor the experience and the same goes for your dogs.

As far as the order In which you feed your dogs, I believe that you can and should vary it. Maybe you think your dogs have some sort of pecking order and you want to reinforce that? Well, there will always be leaders and followers in a multiple dog household, but you are the ultimate leader, not any individual dog. So reinforcing an order that indicates a leader among the dogs can inadvertently cause problems so dispense with that theory. What some call dominance in dogs can be fluid depending on the situation and even the day.

In general, you should feed your dogs in a different order every single time you feed them. There is always the chance that at some point, someone else will be giving your dogs a treat or meal. Do you really want to set into stone that Fifi must get hers first and then

JASMINE, TAKODA, OSKAR & RUBY WAITING TO BE RELEASED TO EAT.

> Varying the sequence order when feeding your dogs will prevent problems down the line.

Fluffy and then so on? What if Fifi suddenly has an inflated sense of her importance due to receiving her meal/treat first and decides to display her irritation at the others when she is not first? If you are not present, will someone who doesn't know the pecking order be equipped to handle the melee that that may follow a sequence error? Should they have to? No, anyone offering your dogs a treat or meal in your absence should simply have the pleasure of offering the goodies and having the dogs receive them graciously! There should be no melee to handle. So mixing up the feeding order on a regular basis is your key to preventing chaos on those unavoidable occasions when someone else will need to feed your crew. The added bonus is that when someone other than you offers your dogs a treat, the dogs will not jostle for attention. Win/win all around, right?

However, as you will see from the examples later in this section, there are exceptions to every rule. If you feel uncomfortable mixing things up, then don't. But do be aware that having a particular order makes things harder for anyone else feeding your dogs as well as yourself. And for safety's sake, have a prominently displayed feeding instruction schedule in your kitchen, should someone else ever need ever to step in. This is the minimum needed to prevent chaos.

Address your dogs' manners when it comes to feedings. If you do not currently require your dogs to sit until you release them in order to receive their dinner, I strongly suggest that you start incorporating this into their daily routine. I cannot stress how much calmer feeding time can be with this simple addition. Of course, some day your dogs will be so well behaved at meal times, there will be no need to do this with each and every meal. But you'll only get there by incorporating some structure from the get go!

As far as the manners go, there are several cues covered in Proofing the Pups but it is by no means all inclusive. For more detailed step-by-step training information, please see the resources section for suggested reading material. If one or more of your dogs is guarding his food, consult a professional.

Some of the cues that come in handy at dinner time are "sit", "stay" and/or "wait", "leave it" and "drop it". I suggest that you train each dog one-on-one to respond to any of the cues as well as teaching them general impulse control. When each dog reliably responds, then you may add one dog at a time and work up to group compliance. This systematic approach will be the same for each type of manners that you need to instill as a group. See the chapter Choreographing the Crew for more on this. It would be mass chaos to expect to train all of your dogs at once en masse. And you certainly don't want mass chaos!

> Serious guarding can include both guarding from the humans or the other dogs, in such a way that you fear being bitten or fear a dog fight occurring. It is important to get professional assistance with this ASAP.

Even after your dogs are trained nicely in mealtime manners as a group, you can't just sit back and relax. Mealtimes are a big deal in a dog's mind. Until you have done this over and over and over and even then, you must always be prepared to step in if need be. Body blocks are a handy thing to use at a moment's notice. Simply stepping in between two dogs where you see potential trouble brewing can sometimes put an immediate stop to it. Stepping in reestablishes you as the benevolent leader and usually sends the potential troublemaker back to his spot if you intervene quickly enough. Quickness is important when you have high-value resources at stake. Make no mistake about meals. Most dogs are serious about their food. Whether they guard or not, they still want their food to remain theirs. As it should!

Is it appropriate for a dog to offer a low growl or a look if another dog wanders into his eating space? Yes, actually it is, within reason. Ideally, however, said dog should not have to growl a warning because you will have seen to it that he is safe to eat his meal in peace. I expect that if you have a dog that would do more than offer a growl or a look to keep his food, then you will address that with the appropriate resources such as a local trainer or well-respected book on the subject, whichever is appropriate for your skill and knowledge level. Likewise, I expect that if you have a dog who thinks that it's okay to look over everyone else's meals, you will take care of training

> Body blocking is exactly what it sounds like. Place your body between two or more dogs to redirect certain scenarios for a better outcome.

an appropriate behavior to replace that one. If it makes everything go more smoothly and this is your only multiple dog worry, then just do feed them all separately.

If you have any doubts as to the behavior you will get during a mealtime, it is REALLY important that you place safety over convenience. Feed separately, tether, etc. Just don't take chances. This is probably the most important issue you could face as a multiple dog owner. How you dispense this valuable resource sets a tone. So set the right tone. As you will read shortly, some owners feed all dogs together and some feed separately for convenience. Whatever works best in your home is what is best for you. If you choose togetherness, choose it because it is safe to do so. And if you have never had issues with mealtimes with your current crew, then don't let me make you paranoid. Just be aware that it isn't always that easy. But if you work at it when need be, once you have a good handle on what to watch for while your crew is having their meals, it will become second nature and you will not need to feel like a foreman watching a potentially wayward employee or two. You will get used to what is okay and what looks sketchy.

Adding a New Dog

When you add a new dog to your life, you should feed that dog separately at first. You will need to gauge his mealtime manners and you certainly don't want your new addition to go rushing at everyone's bowls and cause a mass riot. What I would suggest is a baby gate separating the room where you feed the main group from the room where you'll feed the new dog. You can better gauge how your new addition

> Go slowly when integrating a new dog into your crew with mealtimes.

feels about others near his bowl this way. Make sure that the gate is securely attached and that your main crew will be mannerly towards him and vice versa. Be prepared to step in if need be. You can do this until you feel that your dogs are ready to be combined with the new addition. Even when you combine them all, I suggest that you tether the newbie to something sturdy if you have any questions as to whether he will bother the other dogs while eating. You should always take baby steps when combining new dogs with resident dogs. Taking baby steps ensures you that each step of the process is solid before you proceed with the next step. You will be setting them up for success. You should reward your dogs, new and old, for eating politely in the presence of the others. You should also reward those who finish first yet do not try and police the other dogs' eating habits. Make mealtime a relaxation time for everyone.

Foster Dogs

I do not believe you should combine the feeding place of your own dogs and the foster dogs you may have. As I said previously, I have done it but it caused mealtimes to be too stressful for my own dogs so after an doggy ER visit when Siri got bitten for being too interested in a foster dog's food, the eating arrangements were then separated. If you decide to keep your foster dog, (which many people have done, myself included) then of course you can integrate that dog into the regular feeding regimen. That would be the exception to the rule. But as far as dogs whose tenure in your life is temporary, just don't chance it. It's so much easier on everyone involved to simply have separate feeding places for each. I feed my foster dogs in the foster dog room. I do take their food up first, before I feed my own dogs. Do my dogs notice this? I am sure that they do and I am sure that it likely mildly annoys them at times, but I am equally sure that they understand that our meal times are family time and I want to relax with them, not hop up and feed the foster dog while they are eating.

So in order to facilitate this family time, the foster dog gets his dinner when I am ready to do the final prep on their food, so that my dogs and I all get to eat together. We like it that way. Have I fed my foster dog loose with my dogs in the past? Yes, I have and I have learned from that experience. I have also tethered foster dogs to something and had them eat in the same room as my dogs. But I came to the same conclusion that I did about sleeping arrangements: it's unfair of me to subject my dogs to the stress of having an unknown dog present during these important daily routines. So I allow us the luxury of being a family in those routines.

As mentioned before, there are exceptions to every rule. The breeds that I tend to deal with the most in my home can often have more of a potential to guard than some other breeds. If your breeds or mixes thereof, would not dream of attempting to steal a housemate's food, then by all means feed foster dogs along with resident dogs. Continue with what works well for you. But do be aware that some breeds have this propensity, so if your crew contains a guarder, separate him from the others for mealtimes for safety's sake.

Real Life Mealtimes

As I said, I feed all of my dogs in one room, which is the kitchen. All dogs have their own spot and there are no barricades. They all eat politely and no one drifts, at least not at dinnertime. They eat on towels at dinnertime since I feed the raw diet. (For information on this feeding method, please see the resources section.) But in the morning, the dogs use ceramic bowls since I feed ground meals then. Because the bowls can be mobile when they are pushing their snouts into them, they can drift a bit then, and sometimes they do end up eating closer to each other and all is fine. But we have this down to a science here and it won't automatically be like this in every home! It takes work. After meals, they do go around and lick each other's towels or bowls. This is okay with everyone and I have no problem with it. After their meal, they wait for me to finish my meal and once that happens, I offer each of them a small piece of whatever I was eating. They must behave politely and sit for this, but since we have been together for a while, I no longer ask for sits at dinner. They are all polite about waiting to be fed.

As noted earlier in this section, I mix up the feeding order quite a bit, so that it's rather unpredictable. However, at the time of this writing, my youngest dog, Trent, is a wannabe "ladder climber" without the appropriate leadership skills, so he always gets fed last for now. He does sometimes get treats out of that order, but until he hones his impulse control skills, he will continue to get his meals and treats last, most of the time. As you will read below, others employ this subtle way of sending a message as well.

JOY AND DOUG HAVE EIGHT DOGS whom they feed in a specific order in a specific location. I am naming the dogs below in the order they are fed. Gunnar is the dog most likely to be targeted to be bullied by the other household dogs, and he tends to be a food thief, so he is fed alone in the bathroom. Dan is the second most likely to be picked on and he is a picky eater to boot, so he eats alone in the bedroom and gets approximately 10 minutes to finish or the meal gets picked up. Sierra and Joe are fed together in the kitchen and neither are food thieves but will defend their food if challenged. They finish at the same time so all works out. Rhett is given his bowl just outside the kitchen but generally moves it where he wants within the free area Joy and Doug have established, and he finishes in a timely manner. Aries eats in her crate as she preemptively defends her food from everyone. Brody was an unruly adolescent and grew up with the "Nothing in Life Is Free" leadership program. He is fed next to last in the kitchen, out of habit from this protocol, to emphasize the point that he is not in charge. Since Miss Brandy joined the household, she is now fed last in the guest bedroom for the same reasons as Brody, since she has leadership aspirations that are not to be realized.

JEN AND JEFF FEED THEIR CREW in the living room in this order; Takoda, Oskar, Ruby and Jasmine. All dogs maintain "sits" when given their bowls, until released. Jasmine is fed in increments because she eats too fast. She also sometimes guards Oskar's food from him because he eats at a normal pace. When she does this, she gets relegated to the kitchen to finish her meal.

CHERI AND RUSS FREE FEED THEIR CREW of three. They all share one large bowl and graze at will. When they get special treats, such as ice cream or leftovers, it is divided into three bowls and they all play musical bowls until they decide which bowl they want. Then they eat. They again play musical bowls after they are done, to make sure that all has been eaten. If they are given bones as an after-dinner treat,, each one goes to a different part of the house to chomp on it but there are no issues.

SUE AND LAURA FEED EVERYONE TOGETHER at their own feeding "station". The two boys, Deus and Xander, switch back and forth between bowls on a frequent basis during the meal as well as once they are done, in case one should have something more interesting than the other. The boys weigh almost one hundred pounds more than their canine housemate, Ana, yet they don't bother her feeding station at all, except to sniff around the base for missed morsels when she is done. Miss Ana does dance around their feet when the food is first being passed out but they ignore her, which is fantastic. When Mona was alive (Ana's predecessor), she required special attention at meals so there was more supervision over her food to make sure that the boys were kept away from her while she ate. When it was clear that she was completely finished, the boys were permitted to peruse the leftovers.

LILIAN FEEDS HER THREE DOGS SEPARATELY because they do tussle over food. It's safer and easier to allow them their own spaces, so Titan eats in the kitchen, Phoenix eats in the dining room and JJ eats on his bed in the living room. They all know their own spots and go there at mealtime and wait patiently until it is their turn. She does vary who gets their meal first. She also places their food down in front of them and requires them to wait until she releases them to eat.

CRYSTAL AND ROSS FEED ALMOST EVERYONE TOGETHER, foster dogs and all. She requires a down-stay and that her entire crew be relaxed before getting released to eat. They are then released one at a time to their bowls. When they are done eating, they must resume a down stay because she doesn't want them hovering over each other's bowls. Once they are all done with their meals, they get a cookie and then they are released. Sammy eats on the couch because he's very picky and it takes him forever to eat. If they have any foster dogs who are not ready for the down-stay lineup they crate them for meals.

Providing your dogs with the best nutrition that you can afford will help to build a solid base for a calmer multiple dog home.

These are very different examples of how mealtimes can be handled. Through trial and error, you will find what works best for your crew, but following basic safety instructions will help things to progress more smoothly.

Nutrition and the Multiple Dog Household

As I have mentioned previously, I feed my dogs a raw food diet. I believe that behavior is influenced in part by diet. I like to give my dogs the best basis for a healthy and happy life by taking great care with their diet. I also sometimes make diet a part of the conversations that I have with my clients, both in classes and private consultations. Diet in dogs is much like in humans. If you eat a highly processed diet full of refined sugar and chemical preservatives, you don't feel your best. The same applies to dogs. Of course, there are always those exceptions like Great Aunt Millie, who ate nothing healthy her entire life and lived to a ripe old age of ninety-seven and that dog you knew while growing up who ate nothing but Ole' Roy and lived until the age of seventeen. These are exceptions, not the norm.

The instances of cancer and auto-immune related disorders in dogs are higher now than was years ago. More pets are getting as obese as their owners! This can all be controlled by a healthy diet. What does this have to do with a multiple dog household? Well, diet is a foundation. If you build your foundation carefully, everything else is sturdy. If you provide your dogs with the best nutrition you can afford and take care that they have a healthy and varied diet,

SOME OF THE MAKINGS OF A WELL STOCKED DOG PANTRY.

you are setting the stage for a calmer multiple dog home. Preservatives and sugar can make a dog who is already prone to high energy even more high energy. Multiply that by how many high energy dogs you have and you can see why feeding a more nutritious diet that doesn't add any hyperactivity would be an attractive option!

These are some of the makings of a "stocked cupboard" in my house. The raw items in the photo on the previous page include raw turkey necks and ground raw buffalo. Prepared foods pictured include several grain free biscuits, canned 100% cooked meats (buffalo and rabbit) and canned tripe. My cupboard and refrigerator also usually contains canned fish, both salmon and jack mackerel, raw chicken parts in several forms, ground raw rabbit and goat, I also use eggs, cottage cheese, plain low fat yogurt and kefir, raw liver, Parmesan cheese and vegetables processed in a blender. Supplements chosen for each dog complete the well stocked pantry.

But you don't have to overhaul your kitchen habits to feed your dogs more nutritiously. You have several options. Raw feeding is just one of them. Other options include a home cooked diet, a mixture of home cooked and raw (at different meals), a mixture of either raw or home cooked and premium kibble (again, at different meals) or premium kibble with regular real food add-ins for a nutrition boost. The possibilities are extensive. There are various sources that you can turn to for research purposes, so that you can choose the best option for you and your crew. There is a publication called the Whole Dog Journal that releases a list of best dog foods in February of every year. This same publication offers several articles that are available online for purchase that discuss different feeding methods, along with real life examples. There are also many websites available to read about various methods. One highly recommended website is dogaware.com. The owner of this website, Mary Strauss, also writes periodically for the *Whole Dog Journal.* And there are books galore on these subjects. Some of the best are listed in the reference section.

I strongly urge you to do your research on this subject. You will be amazed at the difference in your dogs in many areas: sparkling eyes, whiter teeth, lustrous coats, lack of the typical dog smell, no mouth odor, better energy levels and a better overall attitude. A foundation of good nutrition will make everyone's life smoother to start with, so you can then rule that out as a possible cause of any issues that still remain. Having really good food available to your dogs may seem at first like you are setting up a situation for resource guarding. Yes, this food will be of a higher value than Ol' Roy™, I cannot lie about that. However, remember the abundance thing that I mentioned previously? A better quality of food will be more satisfying, especially if you choose the raw feeding option. Why? Because quality food satisfies a primal need, simple as that.

And with raw feeding, if you feed your dogs whole pieces of meat, you get the added benefit of hearty chewing to reduce the dogs' anxiety. After a raw dinner, dogs are calmer.

As far as treats are concerned, I am advocating healthy and good tasting treats that don't take anything away from the effort of a nutritious base diet. There are suggestions and recipes in the resource section of this book. Don't waste your time researching and implementing a healthier lifestyle including diet and then use sugar- and preservative-laden supermarket treats. I also believe in using appropriate supplements judiciously. Research your dogs' needs (again, dogaware.com is great for this as well) and choose the right supplements for them. This will enhance their diet and can sometimes mean the difference between a dog that runs around like a puppy and a dog that has creaky knees and has trouble getting up.

Chapter 4

Let Sleeping Dogs Lie
Where Do They All Fit?!

You like having your dogs sleep with you but now you have more dogs than you expected. While many trainers will tell you that it's a bad thing to allow your dogs to sleep with you, I am not one of them, UNLESS you are having compliance issues with a dog or two. Then there are rules. Before I go further, let me further define what I mean by compliance problems. As mentioned previously, compliance problems can include many things, both in and out of the bedroom. One compliance issue includes pushiness. This issue is what keeps one of my dogs from sleeping on the bed at night. Trent takes a mile when you give him an inch and for sleeping purposes, that means he is very pushy with the other dogs on raised surfaces, especially Siri. He doesn't let up on trying to be right in her face to the point of her having to faux growl at him. So he sleeps in the doggy condo corner. He is permitted on the bed during the day. He also has access to couches but he is not always permitted on the couch in the evening if Siri is on there unless he leaves her alone.

> Issues of any kind relating to allowing a dog to sleep on the bed should be cause for the dog in question to lose that privilege. These issues can include but are not limited to: guarding the bed, being impolite on the bed, and refusing to relinquish the bed.

I have increased his privileges as his behavior has improved, but I am not yet completely satisfied with his level of pushiness so sleeping on the bed at bedtime is something he has yet to earn. Siri will help give the heads up when he leaves her alone.

Some very important compliance issues that need to be taken very seriously are guarding any raised surfaces such as beds or couches from human family members or other canine family members. That should automatically lose the dog(s) in question the privilege of being permitted on a couch or a bed at all. The guarding issue needs to be addressed by a professional, so I am not offering a solution to that

> Some signs of canine pushiness include always shoving to the front of the line such as rushing to get through doorways first, trying to get treats first, being too persistent with repeating already interrupted behaviors.

behavior here. But I will strongly emphasize that this should NOT be tolerated at all, by either large or small dogs. Permitting access to couches and beds in cases such as this is VERY dangerous so get some assistance immediately with turning this behavior around. Maybe someday you can have them back on the beds and couches safely but not while guarding is an issue at all.

Keep in mind that this behavior is equally dangerous whether the dog is guarding against humans or other dogs. Even if the dog is only guarding from other dogs in the home rather than you, if the other dog doesn't want to back down, you will have a fight on your hands and is this really what you want to wake up to in the middle of the night? You can get bitten accidentally. Just say no to guarding dogs on beds and couches and get help asap. You will never regret it.

So if you are NOT having compliance problems, there are many scenarios that you can entertain to accommodate your canine family. I am a firm believer that dogs should sleep in the vicinity of their people. Dogs are extremely social creatures and like to feel a part of a social circle. Raymond Coppinger, in his book *Dogs - A Startling New Understanding of Canine Origins*, notes that it is very likely that

> It is imperative that you get immediate professional assistance if you have a dog who is guarding raised surfaces from either human and canine family members.

dogs domesticated themselves. Being social is part of the reason. Although I am not a fan of the wolf model theory as it relates to dogs, one cannot deny the ancestry and the social nature. They do everything as a pack. Sleeping near one another is an important part of that. It's the same with the canines in our lives. They want to be with their crew. You are part of their crew. You are also their leader, which makes you a safety magnet.

All humans in the home are the leaders. So if there are multiple humans in the home, there can be multiple sleeping arrangements, dependent at least partially on who prefers to sleep with whom and what everyone finds the most comfortable. My suggestion in those cases is that the dogs sleep on the same floor/level of the house as the humans, if they want to, that is. Not all dogs will want to sleep where you want them to but if you have no problems with your dogs having full run of the house, even at night, then let them sleep where they are comfortable. It's all one big den to them.

If you are not comfortable with night time run of the house, use baby gates or something similar to block access to areas you want to keep off limits. If it is also necessary to block passage from one room to the next on the sleeping level, that is fine, but choose the dogs that are in certain rooms together carefully according to what is best for everyone involved, human and canine. Perhaps a child is a little too permissive with one dog, but that is their favorite dog. Again, if there are no compliance problems, it's okay, but if there are compliance problems, that dog should not be sleeping with that child.

So where do you put all the dogs, especially when all the humans sleep in the same room? You may be a single person or a part of a couple. Perhaps you have five dogs and a queen size bed? Well, maybe now is the time to peruse the bed sales! But joking aside, just as you want to be comfortable and safe when you sleep, it is very important that your dogs are comfortable and safe when they sleep. If everyone cannot fit on the bed, or

CHASE & SAMMY HAVING A NAP. THIS IS A GOOD EXAMPLE OF A DOG BED SET UP IN THE BEDROOM.

horror of horrors, you are not a dog-on-the-bed kind of person, then by all means, get as many thick comfy dog beds as you can afford. If money is tight, use thickly stacked blankets. The dogs don't know the difference. Thrift shops are great sources for blankets and comforters. Simply launder and stack them and you have instant affordable dog beds!

> Dogs need to be comfortable during sleeping hours, just like humans. Make sure that you provide the comfort that they need in order to get much needed rest.

I have a large bedroom and one entire corner is my "doggy condo corner." I have three large dog beds placed next to one another. Three of my dogs can fit on this set up. If your dogs are smaller, then you can get several in a set up like this. The way it works at my house at the time of this writing is that everyone but the one aforementioned dog is permitted to sleep on the bed at bedtime if they want. Whether they do or not varies by season primarily. I have one dog that will only stay on the bed for a short period, if he gets on at all, and then he chooses his favorite spot of the moment. The spot that he chooses may be the floor, the doggy condo corner, the spare bedroom (if we have no fosters at the moment) or the cool bathroom floor. Another dog always sleeps on the bed unless it's summer. And yet another dog starts or finishes on the bed, again unless it's summertime, and sleeps in various places in between.

MERLIN IN THE DOGGY CONDO CORNER.

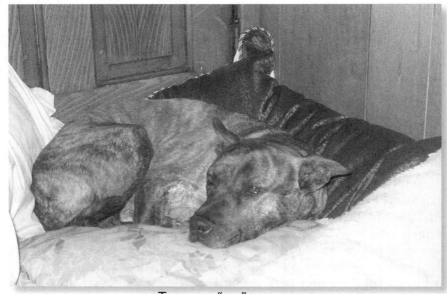

TRENT IN "HIS" CORNER.

The possibilities are endless. Trent likes to sleep in the furthermost dog bed nicely tucked in his corner.

One thing to keep in mind when deciding where to place dog beds in your bedroom is whether your dogs have spatial issues with one another, especially when sleeping. Some dogs have a reflex startle response when being awakened and they can snap without thinking. This can sometimes be breed specific. Other dogs don't do well being touched when resting, even if accidentally, by another dog. It sounds very much like the whole sibling rivalry thing —"mom, he's touching me!" — but it can be dangerous. If this is something you experience with your crew, then spread those dog beds around the room. If the spatial issues are severe, you should, of course, be working with a professional on this but you could also crate the dog that is the worst offender so you don't wake up to any unpleasant and dangerous skirmishes. Breaking up dog fights while wearing your pajamas is not generally on the list of anyone's favorite activities so minimizing this potential is important!

> Scatter dog beds around the bedroom if your dogs are easily startled when sleeping. This minimizes the potential for fights during sleeping hours.

If you have the option of allowing your dogs several rooms on the same floor that the humans sleep on, that may be your best option. If you trust your dogs with the run of the house, then simply let then choose where they sleep, as I mentioned. It's okay if they choose a different floor than you sleep on if you and they are comfortable with this. I have dog beds in almost every room of my house and I strongly believe that there should be dog beds or comfy places they are permitted to use, in each room where the family spends a large amount of time. This gives the dogs a place to call their own and in turn, gives them options for rest periods. So provide comfortable dog beds and/or blankets in each room that they may choose. The spots that they choose during the day may differ from bedtime. Don't try to make them sleep on the bed if they don't want to. And in the same vein, don't try to make them sleep on a dog bed if they prefer the floor. But if they prefer your bed and you prefer they sleep elsewhere, that is perfectly fine. Not everyone is comfortable emotionally and/or physically with their dogs sleeping in bed with them. That is an individual thing. But keep in mind the facts: if they are not comfortable, they won't choose the spot you want them to sleep in, simple as that. This is why the beds/blankets on the floor need to be comfortable to THEM. Giving the dogs options is important, especially if you have all large dogs and a not so large bed.

So if they are on the bed, should you move them around or ask them to get off the bed if you don't have enough room? Absolutely! You are the one who needs to be able to provide for them. You need your beauty sleep. Gently rearrange the sleeping arrangements when need be. Do not give in on that. You are the leader here and you have the opposable thumbs. It is also perfectly fine if you want one dog but not another to sleep on the bed. But don't make that a habit unless that dog is the only one who does not have compliance problems. (If that is the case, you should be working on this issue with the goal of resolving it.)

Keep in mind that playing favorites can be a tricky proposition. There should be a good reason for this and you should not show continued favoritism to one dog all around. It will cause problems between the dogs. That subject is addressed in various chapters but it does have relevance here to be sure. Favored sleeping

> Don't continually play favorites by only permitting one dog on the bed on a regular basis. That can cause problems among the crew.

arrangements are a resource. Be aware that access to any favored resource is something you choose with care. If you prefer only letting one dog on the bed each night, then take turns and everyone else gets comfy dog beds. Rotating privileges is a great way to avoid playing favorites. Did you expect there to be so many subtleties to consider with multiple dogs? Who knew this would need to be so carefully arranged! But don't worry, it will become second nature.

The Older/Infirm Dog

What if you have a dog who for some reason cannot climb stairs well anymore and you sleep upstairs? Well, certainly that is a wrench in the works. But he can adjust if you make provisions for him. If this is a small dog, I recommend that you simply carry your dog upstairs and settle him where it best suits everyone. But that is not quite so easy when that dog is larger, is it? In that case, you have adjustments to make. This is never going to be easy for the dog who is downstairs (unless they preferred this all along) but there are plenty of things that you can do to ease his mind. For a start, make his bed in the room downstairs where you spend the most time. Another option is the spot where he seems to be comfortable most frequently on that floor. Give him the most comfortable bed you can afford.

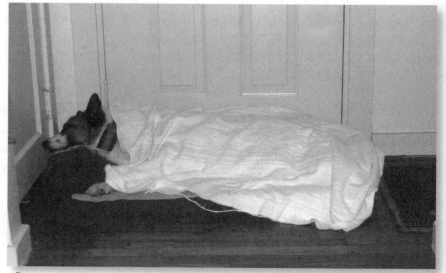

ROCKY IN HIS FAVORITE SPOT. ROCKY WAS IN HIS FINAL YEARS AND COULD NOT CLIMB STAIRS ANYMORE.

Every evening, spray D.A.P. Comfort Zone® on his bedding or if that room is small, you could use a plug in version instead. You can also use various Bach® remedies to ease his worry. I am not going to suggest one single essence over another, as each dog is different, and only someone who knows your dog best can do that. Bach publishes a chart that helps explain the best use of each essence. However I can suggest that you have the Rescue Remedy mixture on hand. That is a nice all-around calming agent that you can try.

Create a bedtime ritual that you share with just this dog. Do not use a baby voice to reassure your dog if he seem anxious about your going upstairs and leaving him. Use a low, calm and confident voice to comfort him. A low radio left on a soothing station may help him sleep. Or a white noise machine may be just the ticket. If your other dogs are tuned into this dog's anxiety, they may "check in" with him to say goodnight. This can include a nudge or a nuzzle. Let them do this as long as it's accept-

SALLY, IN HER SPECIAL AREA, RECOVERING FROM SURGERY.

able to both. The bedtime ritual can be enjoyable for everyone.

One thing that is very important in this situation is that someone upstairs should still be able to hear the dog who is sleeping downstairs if need be. He needs to feel that his needs are still being met.

> For a dog who can no longer sleep on the same level as the others because of physical reasons, be sure to make special arrangements for his emotional and physical comfort.

What if he has to potty in the middle of the night and no one hears him ask? This will only increase his anxiety and make things worse. If it is too hard to hear with just your ears, then invest in an inexpensive baby monitor for this purpose. That way, all his needs are met as best as possible under the circumstances. Along these lines, make sure that you limit his access to things that can harm him in the dark. Keep his sleeping area safe. And when you awake, make sure that he is included with the morning ritual as much as possible so as to ease any additional worries.

SAMMY RECOVERING IN HIS OWN SPECIAL SET-UP DESIGNED TO ENHANCE HIS RECOVERY

To Crate or Not to Crate

You may be reading this and wondering where crates come in, right? Certainly many dogs sleep in their crates as puppies and throughout their lives. That is fine, but for sleeping, your dogs should be comfortable, just like you are in your bed. As I said, I am a fan of the dogs sleeping as near as possible to the humans. So I believe that dogs who do sleep in crates should still be in the bedroom with the humans. If that is not physically possible due to the size of the crates and the size of the room, then as close to the bedroom as possible is ideal.

Again, there should be a bedtime ritual that you work out with your dogs. Make everyone feel like an important part of the family. What if you have one dog sleeping in a crate because he is still a puppy and the others are scattered wherever they want? That's fine! Your goal will be to wean the puppy into a similar arrangement as the rest of the crew. That will come with time. But that crate should be as close as

> Crates that are also used for sleeping should have comfy bedding in them for bedtime. They should be as close as possible to the human sleeping areas. If you crate your dogs during the day, it is advisable to not crate at night. If you are not comfortable with them roaming, consider tethering in the same room a human sleeps in instead. Tethering should always be supervised.

possible to the sleeping room of the humans. I cannot stress this enough. It's bonding time and you are building that bond. You are the benevolent leader, even while you are sleeping. You'd be amazed at the difference this can make in your relationship with your dog. That said, can you still have a strong bond with your dog if that is not the case? Of course, but I believe you will have to work a little harder, that's all.

Foster Dogs

So what do you do if, like me, you have a steady stream of foster dogs in your home? Well, when I was just starting out in rescue, I used to tether them in the same room that my dogs and I sleep in, in the same dog bed corner. However, in time I realized that this practice infringed upon my own dogs rights. How is that possible?

Well, my dogs are my family and just as in a human family, when there are guests in the home, it is important to have a "sacred" place, if you will, where you can relax without any interference. I believe that forcing the foster dogs upon my dogs, in their sleeping area, added stress to their lives.

So I developed a room for the foster dogs. It is actually a guest bedroom so there is a bed that all of the dogs, including a foster

DUSTIN (FOSTER DOG) & KERA ON DUSTIN'S BED, WITH SIRI RELAXING NEARBY.

dog, are permitted on. In fact, that is the only bed that the foster dogs are permitted on. There is a crate as well, which a new dog may sleep in, to be determined by their behavior when they must be left unsupervised. On average, most dogs, even when new, do just fine sleeping on that guest bed. In my case, the guest room is just across the landing from my own bedroom so I can hear a dog if he stirs and needs to go out. If a room you'd like to use is not within hearing distance of your own sleeping space, you might want to confine a foster dog or new crew member to a crate for sleeping. You could also use an x-pen within the larger room.

I strongly believe that a dog that

> If you take foster dogs into your home, make sure that the foster dogs are safe and comfortable during sleeping hours.

is crated for long periods during the day should not also be crated for sleeping. You may have to get creative if that is your situation. Perhaps the baby monitoring system that I mentioned earlier may have an application here as well. You will learn with practice what works best for you. In any case, dogs who is not sleeping in the same room as you or another family member, should most definitely be tired and have had a chance to relieve themselves immediately prior to bedtime. Some form of comfort should be provided to them such as a blanket, a soft toy, a chew type toy, etc. They should also have access to some water, but not a large amount until you know how they handle this.

Just like your older or infirm dog who can no longer sleep on the same level of the home as before, the foster/new dog will also require some special attention prior to retiring for the evening. Care should also be taken to make sure that this dog gets outside to relieve himself in the morning along with everyone else. Establishing a routine will go a long way towards having the new/foster dog be integrated well into your household. Dogs love routine! I cannot say that enough. It helps them feel safe. A dog who feels safe is a happier dog.

I have asked many of my friends how they handle their multiple dog arrangements. Here are some examples of how a wide range of multiple dog owners manage so that you can best decide what works for you.

Real Life Sleeping Arrangements

JOY AND DOUG HAVE A SECTIONAL SOFA in their living room that they have divided with two couches facing each other and a recliner at the end. Brody sleeps on one couch, Rhett sleeps on the other and Brandy sleeps on the recliner. Aries sleeps in her crate in the same room with the crate door open or curled up on a blanket on the back of the one of the couches. Before Joy turns in every night, each dog sleeping in the living room (which is actually within viewing distance from the master bedroom) gets tucked in with a blanket, a kiss and goodnight lovings. If there is any sign of a thunderstorm, Rhett joins them in the bedroom. Even though Rhett, Brody and Brandy are the big "kids" and Aries is a little one, she and Sierra do not get along so Aries does better in this room. In the bedroom, the rest of the little ones; Sierra, Dan, Gunnar and Joe, sleep in bed with the humans, with the most coveted spots being between the pillows or between their legs.

JEN AND JEFF DO NOT HAVE THEIR BEDROOM OPEN TO THE DOGS for allergy reasons. Unless they have a new dog in the house the dogs have their choice of anywhere in the living room to sleep. Ruby sleeps on the dog bed or a blanket pile. Jasmine considers herself too good for anything on the floor level so she is usually either on the futon or the recliner chair. The three large dogs, Takoda, Oskar and Jasmine often trade places every night between the futon and the recliner chair. Two dogs share the futon while the other one gets the recliner!

CHERI AND RUSS GIVE THEIR DOGS THE OPTION of sleeping wherever they want. Delanie likes dark and quiet so she sleeps on a blanket in the back corner of the closet. Socretes loves the fan so he sleeps curled up on the bottom of the bed with the fan blowing on him. Gizmo likes to sleep on his side with his head leaning on something, so he sleeps on a blanket in the corner of the bedroom under the window, he wraps his paws around part of the blanket like he's hugging it and puts the side of his head against the wall. Occasionally Gizmo and Socretes switch places, but Gizmo always has to have his head angled and something in his paws. If he's on the bed, he has his Kong® and his head is on one of the human's feet!

When they had seven dogs, they had a slightly different arrangement. Missy slept stretched out next to Russ with her head on his pillow. Delanie and Fuffers were in the closet together. Killer slept next to the dryer. Dexter always slept on Cheri's side of the bed with her. Bear curled up into a tight ball and slept under the chest of drawers. And Cody, the Rat Terrier, slept under the bed.

SUE AND LAURA'S DOGS ARE ALL IN THE BEDROOM TOGETHER and sleep where they want, sort of! The two boys don't sleep on the bed, or no one else would fit. But little Ana sleeps where ever she wants.

It all works well unless there are guests in the home to disturb the boys (prompting them to start bellowing) or if someone sneaks a Kong® into the room and their surreptitious chewing is keeping others awake.

CRYSTAL AND ROSS HAVE FIVE DOGS *of their own, plus usually at least one foster dog. Dover sleeps in his crate, happily, and so do any foster dogs they have. Sally, Sammy, George and Toby sleep wherever they want, which according to Crystal, means two are on the bed competing with the humans for space and two are nesting on their spots, which include an orthopedic doggy bed and a pile of moldable blankets.*

CHRIS AND MICHAEL HAVE A UNIQUE SOLUTION! *They push a queen and a king mattress together sans box spring, on the floor. They started this when the dogs got older and had trouble getting up onto the bed. Paris usually sleeps on the part of the bed farthest from everyone else. Cherokee either snuggles up by the humans or chooses the dog bed at the foot of the human bed. Apache is tethered to Chris while sleeping as he is still being potty trained. He gets to snuggle close to her because of this. They have done this with up to four dogs in the past.*

LILIAN PROVIDES LOTS OF OPTIONS FOR BEDTIME. *She has three dog beds in her room all spread apart. JJ sleeps on the bed when he is not trying to guard the bed from the cats. He is banished to a dog bed when he does that! Phoenix is too lazy to climb onto the bed so he sleeps on a dog bed on Lilian's side of the bed. Titan is not as interested in cuddling as the other dogs so he usually chooses to sleep downstairs. But sometimes he comes up to the bed for morning snuggles. Her foster dogs sleep either in a crate in a room adjacent to the master bedroom or on a dog bed while tethered to her bed, or once they've earned it, wherever they want.*

SUSAN'S DOGS SLEEP ON DOG BEDS *scattered about her bedroom. She doesn't permit her dogs on the bed.*

As you can see from these examples, there are plenty of solutions to fitting everyone in where they need to be! Get creative, be patient, create a routine and maintain your leadership, even in the sleeping quarters. Remember, prime sleeping spots are resources and everything that is a resource can cause an issue in a multiple dog home. As long as you keep that in mind, you are already a step ahead of them.

Establishing a routine as soon as possible when you have a new arrival is also the fastest way to sleeping harmony. You may have noticed that many of these folks have a bedtime ritual where they say goodnight to each dog. This can be very important. It also serves as a cue to them that it's time to rest and recharge. You will then be even more aware of differences in behavior that may mean one dog has digestive issues or something else is awry and needs attention. Dogs like routine. And dogs LOVE to sleep, so if you have a dog acting differently at bedtime, when said dog has been just fine any other bedtime, pay attention and tune into what they are trying to say.

Chapter 5

Since You've Been Gone
When the Crew is Home Alone

So, where do you want your crew to hang out when the humans are gone? Well, much depends on at what point you are in your multiple dog life. If you have had a successful duo, trio or more and have not crated or separated anyone and all has been well, that's great. Don't change what isn't broken. But if you have recently added a new dog or even more than one new dog or if you are about to, then you cannot simply expect the new dog(s) to blend in with the resident dogs without an adjustment period. And part of this adjustment period means separating the new dogs from the resident dogs when there is no responsible adult human at home to properly supervise.

This is a management technique meant to be used while you are evaluating and integrating the mix. This is an important part of the trust in your leadership that I have mentioned previously. Anything can and might happen when you leave it to chance; there should be no chance if you can help it. Keep the crew who trusts in you safe. Remember, safety is an important resource that your dogs depend on you to provide, so separation of new dogs and resident

> When you add a new dog to your crew, separate the newbie from the resident crew when home alone. Work towards integration slowly so that the safety of all is ensured. Crating a new addition when home alone is the best option until you are comfortable with his behavior. The crate of a newcomer should not be in the same area as the rest of the dogs if they are loose in the house. Block off access to a calm safe room.

dogs is necessary until you are comfortable leaving all your dogs together without worrying what might happen if you ran down the street for a moment. You will know when the mixed group can be trusted to be left alone together when you are not home. And in some cases, the answer may be never. But if integration is to happen, you must move towards this goal incrementally.

First let's address crating. If you already crate any of your dogs, then it's a short leap to crating the new dog until you are comfortable with his behavior. Where should you put a new dog's crate? That depends on where your other dogs' crates are currently placed. It's okay if all the crates are in the same room and it's okay if they aren't. I have a preference for placing crates near one another for dogs who are close to one another. Crates should be located in a calm place; a place where your dogs are used to spending time but not where they would be exposed to a lot of distractions coming from outside of the home. Consider each placement carefully.

Use whatever procedure you already use in getting the dogs into their crates when you are leaving, provided it is a positive procedure, that is! You want the dogs to think of their crates as happy places. If you are unfamiliar with crate training, then you will need to get more familiar with it. It's not hard to learn and you will never be sorry that you made a crate a happy place for your crew. Everyone should get a Kong® or another safe interactive toy in their crate. Make the new dog part of the routine and that will help him to bond with the crew as a whole.

What do you do if you no longer use crates? Can you crate one dog (the new one)? Absolutely! If you are not certain how they will behave together, you should crate the new dog to keep all the dogs safe. Should the crate be in the same room with the resident crew? Professional opinions vary; I say no, not at first anyway. Why take chances? Crates are not foolproof. Sadly, I know of dogs getting out of crates and fighting with housemates they got along with practically every other moment but this one time. With no one home, there were tragic consequences. In addition to potential crate breakouts, resident dogs can also get close to the crate and cause anxiety in the crated dog. Don't take chances. It's just not worth it until you are better able to gauge the compatibility issue.

I strongly believe that a crate for a new dog should be in a separate room where it is not able to be reached by the other dogs. You can close doors between the room with the crated dog at first and graduate to baby gates at some safer point in time. If you have previously given your dogs complete access to your house when they were alone, make sure you don't choose your dogs' favorite room for the new dog's crate. Doing so would definitely create discord. Consider carefully these home alone accommodations and try to treat the dogs equally to provide for their physical and emotional comfort.

Every dog and every group of dogs has a different dynamic, so I cannot give you a timeline for integrating everyone together. No one can decide this but you. You should base your decision on a number of factors: how smoothly is everyone blending together? What stage of alone accommodations worked for your crew before the newcomer? How well-trained and well-behaved are all of the dogs, old and new? If all is going well between everyone and your newcomer is well-behaved and polite, then it might be no time at all before they are all together. But by no time, I mean at least a few months. Honestly, you cannot be too careful when it comes to integration and safety.

In addition to the previous criteria that I mentioned, you should also be aware of potential same sex issues among many breeds as well as between similar age groups. I discuss this further in *And Puppy Makes Three*. Some breeds have known behavior issues between same sexes, most frequently with males, but females are not exempt. Often, these issues become more pronounced when you have two dogs that are near each other in age.

If you have not researched your new dog's breed either before or after adding a new dog, then do so now. Take into consideration your resident crew's breed or breeds. What do you do if you have no idea of the true parentage of your crew? Base your research on the breed they most resemble physically. Sometimes their personality traits take after a breed that is in the mix but less obvious, and with a mixed breed dog, you may be in for a surprise. Some vets now offer a lab test to determine your dog's breed mix if

> Get familiar with the breed traits of your dogs in regards to how they interact with other dogs of the same sex. This is especially crucial to home alone time when combining a new dog with resident dogs in the house.

you are very curious. Regardless of how you proceed, it's good to learn as much as you can about your dogs' natural temperaments.

This is especially important if you currently have a male and a female and are making an addition. Obviously, that will result in having two dogs of the same sex. Tilting the balance can often spur problems for many reasons. It's actually easier to have three mellow males than two confident males and a female. That can be a recipe for trouble, so supervising all interactions are crucial. If you already have two dogs of the same sex and have had no problems, you are probably wondering what the big deal is. Consider yourself lucky. It isn't always that easy and it's better to be prepared and educated. You can refer to the chapter on trouble signs for what to watch for, but researching the breeds that you have and knowing their quirks is step one. Training, training and more training is step two.

Is it easier to have multiple males or vice versa? Either one can be a cake walk or a nightmare. It varies and again, many factors determine whether it's the former or the latter. That's not as helpful as it could be, I realize. But my point is that you should consider breed and sex carefully. I personally have two females and two males and all are guarding/working breeds. Guarding and working breeds are known to have a high instance of same sex aggression. One of my males is very intolerant of any obnoxious behavior of younger males so I must watch him very carefully when I have young male foster dogs. I would never leave a young male foster dog alone with him or even my other more tolerant male. And all of my dogs are trained to be polite with visiting dogs. Consider carefully whether you would want to engage in such vigilance as you integrate new dogs into your household.

Now that you've been considering your dogs' individual natures and the group dynamic, let's continue our discussion about leaving them home alone. I recommend creating a bonding routine to use when you are leaving. Use this same bonding routine with the new dog, even if they are housed in a different area of your home when you leave. You can still continue with a routine and bond with each of the dogs with this routine when you are ready to leave. This routine can include a key phrase you use when leaving as well as the passing out of Kongs® or other mental stimulation toys/treats that are safe to supply your dogs with when alone.

How should you pass them out? I believe that giving the new

dog his Kong® and settling him into his crate before you settle the resident dogs, is best for what I want. But your needs may differ. What do I want? Well, what I want is to reassure my resident crew that just because we have a new personality in our home does not mean that I am replacing them, so I choose to spend a bit more time settling them in before I leave. I take care of the newest addition first, but spend more time with my resident crew. This allows them to have the last goodbyes before I leave.

Similarly at mealtimes, when I prefer that meals be family time, I give the newest dog his meal first. And let's not forget what I said previously about mixing up the order of treats and dinner, etc., okay? When you give the new rival for attention his Kong® first, treat this as no big deal. It should be so commonplace that your crew doesn't get ruffled by it at all. I also do this with foster dogs, simply because I want to spend the last moments before I leave with the ones I love the most. This is not to say that you won't love the new addition; of course you do and will. But during this getting-to-know-you period you may want to spend time prior to leaving, saying goodbyes to the new dog first, with the eventual aim of saying goodbye to everyone together. But in that initial period, I think your resident crew will feel safer in your affection when they see you last thing before leaving. Your experience may differ, so trust your instincts.

As for accommodations, once again, it's very important to keep everyone safe physically as well as emotionally, so separate is best. Follow all of the general rules of basic leaving-the-dog-alone care with the new dog as though he were the only dog. Crate him if you feel it's needed (and I strongly favor this until you know for sure). Or create a dog-safe room with lots of safe toys to keep him busy until you return if you are comfortable with this option. When you return, who do you go to first? I always let the resident crew out first and then get the newbie or foster dog. Of course, everyone heads out to relieve themselves at the same time.

What do I do with my own dogs when I'm gone? When Merlin and Kera were both puppies at the same time, they were crated next to each other in my bedroom. I gradually

> Create a familiar bonding ritual with your dogs for leaving the house. Remember, dogs like routines. Include any new dogs in this ritual. Choose a key phrase if it helps both you and your crew.

gave them more time out of the crate when I wasn't home. I limited their area to two rooms so they had less to guard. That often helps with guarding breeds. But when they destroyed things, they did so as a team, so be aware that more dogs mean more stuff destroyed. There really is a pack mentality of sorts. When they had a lapse in judgment, it was back to crating for a few days.

Although my dogs are trustworthy when they have the run of the house, I have learned that they seem to be less stressed when they have less to guard. Guarding and working breeds tend to be higher-strung about noises than some breeds, so I give them less to guard. My bedroom is the quietest room in my house and it's their safe place room. When most

> If it is too anxiety creating to leave your dogs with full run of the house, simply limit their access to a few rooms that comfort them.

of them were crated, they were crated in that room. None of them needs to be crated now and all four get along great, so they stay together in my bedroom with the door closed and either a radio on or the TV on.

I spray Chill Out before I leave. If storms are predicted, I give Siri, who is not fond of storms, some Bach Mimulus®, and I also spray Comfort Zone® spray on the carpeting. If it is warm out, I leave the overhead fan on and possibly the air conditioner fan. I give them all filled Kongs® and I take their collars off. They go outside the last thing before I leave and then head straight upstairs to

Use natural calming remedies to assist with home alone time if need be, especially when adding a new dog to your crew. Acting low key and nonchalant about departures will help relay that feeling to yours dogs as well. Kongs® are an important addition to your home alone repertoire. If you do not know what a Kong® is, immediately go to your local pet supply store and check them out. Purchase a Kong® for each dog and learn to get creative with stuffing them. Once you discover their power over your crew, you will always wonder how you lived without this wonderful invention. I would do an injustice to them by trying to fully describe what they are so I will simply describe them as a rubber toy that can be stuffed with food to stimulate your dog's brain and satisfy his desire to chew.

take their positions for their Kongs®. Dogs like routine, so this helps them to adjust well because they know what to expect. They enjoy knowing what to expect and are happy to have a regular position to receive their Kong®. It was not always this smooth.

I started with just Merlin and Kera in this present home. I added Siri as a foster puppy (along with her siblings) when the older two were three years of age. When I decided to keep her, at first I crated her in the bedroom with the two older dogs. I already knew that they adored her and she was very young at that time. Eventually, I trusted her to be out of the crate with the two older dogs on short trips and she earned her way to staying out of the crate full time. When I first got Trent, he was crated in the dog room (spare bedroom) and then allowed to be free in that room after increasingly longer test periods.

When it became clear that Trent was staying, I first tested him in the bedroom with the rest on short trips, and it became a permanent situation when we got a new foster dog and Trent could no longer be in the dog room. We never looked back. It worked well. So you see, none of this happened overnight. It was a gradual process and safety was a key factor in every transition. Merlin is not always welcoming every moment of the time to other males, so I took extreme care when integrating Trent into the bedroom accommodations.

Having said this, there are times that I know I won't be gone long (for me, that time could be anywhere from thirty minutes to two hours, maximum, and that is usually unexpected!). So I leave them with the run of the house. From what I can tell, they pretty much hang out in the kitchen and await my return. I might give them a stuffed Kong® bone when I leave like this but then again, if I just expect to run across the street to a relative's house to drop something off, then I might just say "wait, I'll be back" and leave. I think that it's important to have a key phrase that you use when you leave, as it gives them information that helps them feel more comfortable.

Should you do anything differently if you are taking one dog with you and the rest are staying behind? Well, that will depend on your dogs but on average, the only thing I do differently is leave the collar on the dog in question and skip that dog's turn when I am doling out the Kongs®. The dog who is coming along usually has figured out that he is coming with me because he is stil wearing a collar. He will still take his position for the Kong® and then I call his name when I am ready to close the door.

I have found that this keeps my departure with a single dog much more low key than it could be, and low key is what I aim for. The dogs remaining behind always look at me a bit longer than normally before attending to their Kongs® but they will consider it a normal occurrence as long as you do. Dogs take quite a few of their cues from us so be low key and you will usually have low key. Make sure that you take each of them one-on-one with you regularly and this will be normal to them and will not cause jealousy. We will cover multiple dog outings in "Taking it on the Road".

Here are some examples of how others handle leaving their dogs home alone.

Real Life Home Alone

JEN AND JEFF GIVE TAKODA, OSKAR AND JASMINE *run of most of the house when they are gone. They do close the doors to the bedroom and bathroom so the dogs have no access there. Oscar is young and started out confined in the laundry room, then was gradually left out for longer periods so he is good with the freedom now. Ruby, on the other hand, is not trustworthy in her bathroom habits yet so she is confined to the laundry room with a baby gate.*

CHRIS AND MICHAEL HAVE HAD SEVERAL GROUPS *of multiple dogs at a time. When all dogs are potty trained, they have the run of the house and a TV or radio is left on. When their now-deceased Mickey was alive, she had incontinence problems later in life, so they gated her in the kitchen with her dog bed so it was easier to clean, but the other dogs could interact with her across the gate. Now that they have a puppy, he is crated until he is house trained. Once he is house trained, he will be permitted to be out with the other dogs for short periods of time gradually growing longer, when the humans are gone.*

JOY AND DOUG HAVE THREE AREAS THAT THEY USE *for three groups with a total of eight dogs home alone. Sierra is by herself in a spare bedroom. Rhett and Brandy are in the main bedroom and a bathroom together. Brody, Dan, Gunnar, Joe and Aries have the living room and kitchen. Aries also has a crate in this area that she can go into if she desires. The three areas are separated by baby gates and there are two baby gates separating Sierra from where Aries is, as they do not get along at all. All of these dogs respect the baby gates.*

LILIAN'S DOGS HAVE THE RUN OF THE HOUSE *now, but when any of them were new to the crew, they were crated in either the living room or the dining room. Her foster dogs are always crated when she is gone. All dogs, including foster dogs, get frozen stuffed Kongs® or bones. Her own dogs have their regular spots where they go when she is ready to leave, to receive their Kongs®. This makes leaving much easier!*

These are excellent examples of different strokes for different folks. Learn what works for you. Also keep in mind your own crew's individual quirks. Not all dogs respect barriers such as baby gates. Some need closed doors. Some are fine with baby gates some days and other days, they will leap right over them! You just have to be prepared for surprises. I also pay attention to moon and planetary activity, as studies support the effects of lunar activity on dog (and human!) behavior. I am very aware of full and new moon phases as well as some varying planetary activity such as eclipses, meteor showers, etc. During these times, I take extra steps to mitigate any unusual behavior, such as leaving extra toys out, making sure that I have picked up everything that might be tempting, and using extra natural calming remedies.

> Be aware of lunar activity when deciding to allow a new crew member access to the residents when home alone for the first time.

So if you have dogs that sometimes respect baby gates and sometimes don't, pay attention to lunar and planetary activity and during these times. Don't take chances that the baby gate will keep two sometimes feuding dogs apart. Better safe than sorry. Avoid leaving a new dog out for the first time with the resident crew during such times. Take few if any chances during these times. Give out better Kongs®. Make things more dog friendly and make the house peaceful.

To Kennel or not to Kennel

What if you are going away and the dogs can't come? What to do? If this is standard operating procedure, then obviously, you have it covered so skip this section. If this will be your first trip since having multiple dogs, then you need to plan this well in advance if you expect everything to progress smoothly. There are plenty of kennels who will give a multiple-dog discount and understand the needs of kenneling multiple-dogs. Make sure that you do your research and locate them. If you find a gem, don't worry about driving a bit farther. Depending on how many dogs you have total, you may want to consider having more than one to each kennel. Letting dogs who are buddies bunk together often minimizes their stress levels, provided they are not going to cause chaos. When choosing a kennel, consider choosing one that is familiar and comfortable with the breeds that you have. This is another consideration that minimizes chaos.

If you have not kenneled these dogs before, it's a great idea to have a test run. Take them all for day care if the facility offers that option. Then take them all for one overnight. That way they will have already spent time there and know you will come back for them. This is a situation where all of those calming agents that I mentioned previously can be used. Having something that smells of you or other family members as well as their favorite interactive toys is a good idea. All in all, I much prefer kennels that take the dogs out to potty and play rather than a kennel that has an indoor/outdoor run. In my personal experience, many dogs just don't understand the indoor/outdoor concept and some will even hold their excretions as long as they can, making themselves sick in the process.

You will feel much better leaving your crew in someone else's care if you have been reassured that their routine is as close to normal as can be attained in a kennel. Visit and meet them and make sure they understand your breeds. You won't be sorry for the time that this takes.

Another option is having an overnight pet sitter stay at your home while you are gone. If you have that option in your area, it will be much easier on you and your crew, and it tends to be easier to check in on them while you are away! Again, do some research so that you make sure that you make a reliable and safe choice for your crew. This option tends to be more economical for the multiple-dog owner. And since the dogs can stay in their own home, they may have an almost normal routine. As long as you get a reliable and experienced pet sitter who follows your instructions, the chances that this arrangement would cause a problem would be minimal.

> Research the best options for your crew when leaving them behind while you travel. For some dogs, kenneling at a responsible facility will work best. For others, staying in their own home with a petsitter will be much more comforting. With both scenarios, make sure you are fully informed about to whom you entrust your crew. Leave thorough instructions as well as contact info for yourself and a trusted person who is close by.

This is also a really good option if, like me, you are reluctant to over-vaccinate your dogs. Pet sitters don't care if your dogs have a bordatella shot. Just make sure that the pet sitter that you hire will also be there a reasonable amount during the day as well. At the minimum, they should try to adhere to the schedule your dogs would experience while you are at work. This should all be included in the same negotiated price.

All your work at not playing favorites during feeding and treat dispensing times will come in handy now! Few people outside of a home are going to remember specific feeding or treating orders so having someone else feed your dogs will be a breeze since you have set them up to not care who eats first.

If you choose a pet sitter instead of a kennel, then make sure you thoroughly write up any instructions that your pet sitter may need. Having multiple dogs means more work for the pet sitter, too, so make it easier on them by putting it all down in black and white. Have the pet sitter come by and meet your crew before you leave, more than once if possible, so you can see whether the sitter and your crew are a good fit. In addition to being reliable, your sitter should also be familiar with the breeds or mixes of your dogs if possible. As noted before, different breeds of dogs have different personalities, and a good sitter's knowledge of your breeds peculiarities can be helpful. When you are far away from home, do everything you can to avoid surprises.

Chapter 6

Taking It On The Road
Staying Upright While Group Walking!

I will assume that you want to make sure that all of your dogs are properly exercised but that you also don't want to spend every moment walking them. Can you walk them in a group? I am here to say that even if you are a small person who has large dogs, you can eventually do this, if you want to. The key word here is eventually. Walking all of your dogs at one time will take time and effort. I walk a minimum of three dogs at once and sometimes I walk all four. I should also mention that I walk them on leash because I currently live in the city. At the time of this writing, I have four large dogs of varying sizes, from fifty-two pounds to ninety pounds and I do walk all of them at once several times a week. I am a small person who just reaches five feet tall.

As I have mentioned previously, I have one dog who is a work-in-progress and can sometimes be reactive when on-leash. So I can't lie and say it's all sunshine and roses on these walks all the time. But when I practice what I preach, the walk goes well with no teeth-grinding

Management tools can make a multiple dog walk much easier, but they are not a substitute for all important training. If you are grinding your teeth more often than smiling while walking more than one dog at a time, it's time to focus on training and save the multiple dog walks for later! If your teeth grinding is at a minimum, then investigate these management tools to see if they can assist until the training is proofed:

-Head halters

-Front clip harnesses

-Martingales

on my part. Of course, when I walk all four at once, I make slight adjustments in our routine and add some management tools. My dog in-transition, Trent, uses a head halter when on a group walk. I personally use the Premier Gentle Leader® head halter as I feel it is the most easily fitted of the head halters that I have tried. A head halter is not a management tool that I use on a frequent basis otherwise but it can give you more control in situations such as this.

KERA, MERLIN AND SIRI PAYING ATTENTION. TRENT (FRONT) BEING TRENT.

My other three dogs wear just their regular, everyday Martingale style collars in any situation. When I walk Trent by himself or with a foster dog, he wears a front clip harness. I personally favor the Premier Gentle Leader® Easy Walk™ front clip harness. I have found that it is the best fitting of the front clip harnesses for most dogs, especially medium-to-large dogs with large chests, which describes

Trent. As mentioned previously, Trent uses a head halter for group walks which gives me better control; he is simply too often aroused and distracted when with the other dogs for me to leave things to chance.

Teaching a group of dogs to walk with you on a loose leash so that your walk is pleasant may be the hardest exercise that you will face, in my opinion. Of course, some who read that statement will wonder what all the fuss is about. Possibly your dogs are fine on a walk. To you I say, great! You are doing a great job. Make sure it stays that way. But for the rest of you, I suggest that you spend a lot of time in the beginning making it very clear that no forward progress will happen unless your dogs remember that someone is actually holding the leash—you! You will, again, need to teach this individually first and then in a group. At first and even for a while, it is perfectly reasonable to use management tools such as head halters and front clip harnesses on any and all of the dogs.

KIRA, NANOOK, KEEMA AND SCOTT TAKE A WALK. KEEMA ONLY HAS EYES FOR HER DAD.

You may have one dog that is all about you on a walk or anywhere for that matter and that dog doesn't pull at all. That's great; just use a regular buckle collar or a Martingale style limited slip (I prefer these for safety) collar on that dog. Here is another taste of the "life is not fair" concept among your dogs. The others will see fewer restrictions on the more compliant dog as far as body wear and wonder what's up. Anthropomorphizing? Maybe, but personally I don't think so. I place this one in the "learn by watching" column.

Your job, in addition to being very consistent on walks and not allowing forward movement for pulling, is to make sure that you are very positive verbally when rewarding the compliant dog for the good behavior that you would like the other dogs to emulate. When I first taught my older three dogs to loose leash walk, I spent many walks in the woods just standing there waiting for them to stop and turn around and check in with me so I could reward that. That helped them to refocus and remember that I was there, holding the leash.

> It's no easy task to teach one dog to loose leash walk. It's even harder to teach a multiple dog crew. The first rule for each is the same. Not permitting any forward movement when there is a taut leash is the key. Consistency with this rule is one of the most potent training lessons you can pass along to your dogs.

I learned this from the very wise Suzanne Clothier and her life changing book *Bones Would Rain from the Sky*. All that time spent waiting to reward was well worth it. My dogs almost never pull on the leash now. Yes, they ARE dogs and when they get wind of a scent or a sight that is simply too enticing to ignore or if a squirrel teases them right in front of their faces, they briefly pull. So of course, when they do, I go back to what worked. No leash jerking! I don't condone leash jerking. Not only does this just teach them to jerk back (opposition reflex) but it also teaches that you are sometimes scary and cause pain on walks. It can also give them a bad association with whatever they saw when the jerk transpired.

Develop the best relationship that you can with each member of your crew and teaching them to walk as a group will go smoother. A solid relationship will go the farthest towards having your dogs think you are the best thing since sliced liver, even on a walk with tons of distractions. It is up to you to teach your dogs that the fun is always with you. This may seem frustrating at first, especially when you are competing with all of the distractions of the outside world, but you will not be sorry that you invested the time needed to make this point to your dogs.

The relationship-building begins before you ever step out the door to take that walk. At this point, you may be getting tired of hearing me mention it but I cannot stress how important this is. The connection that you build with your dogs is your key to the smoothest running crew of multiple dogs, inside and out. How can you cement this when you are on a walk? Simple. Every single time one of your dogs looks your way when you are out walking, even slightly, acknowledge it. Mark it verbally or with a clicker and treat as often as possible (every time if you are using a clicker!). Be their cheerleader when you do this. Make it a big party. Make them glad that they looked at you.

> Every single time you acknowledge any of your crew member's attention on you, while out and about, is like a deposit into the bank of good things that your dog associates with you. Make this a pleasant and memorable experience and you will increase this activity. This makes for a happier walk for all. Making sure that you carry high value treats with you on group walks will help you to become much more interesting than all of the outside distractions on a much faster basis than without.

Give them what they like. Periodically, when they are ahead of you or looking away, back up and call them happily to you and count to fifteen seconds and during that fifteen seconds have another impromptu dog party.

Should you carry treats with you on walks? I am a big believer in doing so for training a single dog to focus on his owner during walks, so I cannot even stress how much more important it becomes when you are walking multiple dogs. Perhaps you are wondering why you will be tied to carrying treats on walks? Well, look at it this way: do you go to work without being paid? The walking part of the multiple dog equation will be your biggest challenge. Expecting this to happen easily without food rewards is unrealistic, especially during the initial training period.

If you want to do single dog walking, despite having multiple dogs, then you have a much better chance of walking treat-free. But when you walk the crew together, you get the crew mentality. The dogs have more to stimulate them and you become less noticeable, especially if something more exciting is going on. The possibility of getting a special treat for compliance when you are out on a walk is the biggest incentive your dog has to pay attention. But the treats should be used as a reward, never as a bribe. To learn the difference, read the Proofing the Pups chapter. Don't forget to do individual one-on-one training before you take everyone all at once— unless of course, you thrive on chaos and challenges!

Here is my walk prep list for a three-dog walk. Get the treat bag out of the fridge and fill it up with high-value treats. Add poop bags to the key ring on the treat bag. Fill a large bottle of water and grab the collapsible bowl for after the walk. Grab the clicker on a lanyard. Get car keys and leashes. Spray Chill Out on the way out the door and off we go. The additions for a four-dog walk are a Gentle Leader® head halter for Trent and sometimes I dose him with Bach's Elm Flower Remedy® before we leave. To the clicker on a lanyard, which I wear around my neck, I add a whistle for after walk off-leash runs (again, Trent is the one who may need this). With a four-dog walk, I also take a fifty foot long line should Trent's off-leash compliance be off kilter that day.

No dog gets a leash attached to them unless they are sitting. This is second nature for my dogs now so they almost always offer the sit. Thankfully, the days when they all jumped around like idiots upon seeing the leashes come out are mostly gone. I say mostly because every day, my ten-year-old Merlin acts like it's the only day per year he ever gets to go anywhere, at least briefly now!

Teaching this to your crew is not hard. It really only takes one good session to teach this behavior to each dog individually and then as a group. I even teach this to foster dogs that I walk and I walk almost all of them. Be patient and don't attempt this when you are crunched for time, especially your first attempt to do this as a group. Each dog should be well-trained to sit before you do try this. Reach for your dog with the leash in hand, and every time he gets up, the leash comes back to you. Attaching the leash is the reward. It's the same theory as a "wait" at the door. And of course, every step of this process to get them to the car or out onto the sidewalk gives you an opportunity to reinforce this behavior. Sit for every step. Do this and you have a nice foundation for group walks!

Every time I unload the dogs at our walking area, Trent is always last and has to offer a "down" for every privilege, including getting out of the SUV and getting his leash taken off when we reach that point. I verbally reward him for every calm walking moment and every time he turns my way. If he is especially compliant when on a group walk, he gets a treat. (they all do) If he offers another "down" during the walk, all the better. The other three get lots of verbal rewards for checking in and random treats. If a squirrel or deer distract them, whoever does a "watch" first, gets the best treats. All dogs get rewarded for compliance, however.

> High distraction scenarios will differ by the dog. You will either already know or come to know what sets each of your crew off outdoors as well as at what distance you can be from the distraction before one of your crew members react. It is important to know this info so that you can go forth with making your multiple dog walk a safer and more pleasant experience for all of you.

Merlin barely glances at squirrels and other wildlife now as he is far more interested in the food! If my "squirrel and deer screamer" Siri, finds retaining her "watch" harder than usual, I will add several "touch" cues to help her to refocus, as she likes that best. If a dog is rude (usually Siri) about the treat and nudges me or noses around looking for the treat bag, she will get hers after everyone else has had theirs and she will have to work harder for it, again with more cues. I never reward too much eagerness for treats. I want the treat to be a reward, not a bribe.

As far as using the clicker on walks, I use it to mark behaviors that I want more of in a high distraction scenario. It is particularly helpful for anything that your dog may find too fascinating. We play the "Look at That!" game. For more information on how to use the clicker to promote positive associations with high arousal distractions, refer to Leslie McDevitt's book *Control Unleashed* in the resources section. I am very careful not to overuse my clicker for cues they already know very well. I want it to remain an important marker so that they pay attention better. It is very useful on multiple dog walks when a "yes!" marker would go in one ear and out the other.

The clicker cuts through everything.

I have taught my dogs several cues that are handy out on walks, such as "gee" and "haw" which are mushing cues meaning "move right" and "move left" (of me, the handler). I have taught them "front" for "get in front of me" because I don't like having the leash slapping

SIRI DEMONSTRATING A "FIX" WHILE THE OTHERS STROLL ALONG.

the backs of my legs. I have taught them to untangle their own leashes from their legs, both by cue and of their own volition before I have to cue them. This cue is "fix". They lift their legs up and get out of the way of the leash. Of course, they know "over", "up", "off", "come" and all basic cues such as "sit" that would apply outside. I use "look at that" relatively frequently or even just click and treat for calmly looking at things such as bikes, joggers, oddly gated people and other dogs without being cued.

That exercise, (Look at That!) has been the fastest fix for many forms of on and off leash reactivity, in my experience. If you have not read *Control Unleashed*, I strongly recommend it. It will have many uses when assisting with training dogs with any reactivity, but I find it especially helps with a multi-dog household. Another wonderful book that focuses on a more multi-leveled reactivity in dogs based on fear, is *Scaredy Dog!* by Ali Brown. This book is invaluable for working with dogs who have a hair-trigger reactivity. You will find these and other book suggestions in the reference section of this book if this is a concern that you have with your crew.

One of the more interesting things I do with my dogs as a group happens while we are en route to our favorite park. My White Shepherd mix, Kera, loves to bark at anything from inside the car, especially other dogs. It's her only vice. Every time we pass a dog and she barks, I reward the other two dogs and use a No Reward Marker on her, which is a phrase that basically means "you screwed up!" My No Reward marker is "too bad!" said in a happy voice. The next dog we drive by, she remains quiet, and everyone gets a "yay!" and a treat. I do that when I have all four dogs with me as well, but Trent is even more of a vehicle barker, so Kera is relegated to second fiddle barking status. Then we are all just very happy when Trent doesn't bark. We have a big party for that! A product that can be very helpful with some car reactivity is a Calming Cap™, by Premier Products.

> Having a wide repertoire of cues that your crew easily understands will help you in every situation but the great outdoors will be your biggest challenge. When practiced enough to make them reliable in every area, these cues will become invaluable outdoors.

One relaxation exercise that I have found to be very helpful is Dr. Karen Overall's Relaxation Protocol (RP). Basically, this exercise provides your dogs with a default relaxation activity to help them regain calm when they are out of control. It can help you carve calm out of chaos. I have used this with Trent outside in places we go on walks, when no one is around. Although the protocol is meant to be started in the house and expanded upon, Trent is fine and completely relaxed in the house, so we started outside. We graduated to the SUV as that

> The Relaxation Protocol is one of the best tools that you can use to assist any of your crew members to learn to relax in any situation. How to locate this gem on the internet will be included in the References.

is where his explosions typically take place. The RP has drastically reduced his reactivity on leash, along with the "look at that" cue and a "walk away" cue. It is a good idea to have a wide repertoire of cues and actions that you can use if you have a reactive dog of any kind, especially if you plan to walk your whole crew all at once!

While you are training your dogs to walk together safely and calmly, you might want to stick to less populated walking areas and/or less busy time frames. You can gradually work up to walking in busier places and at busier times but the more frequently you permit your dogs to practice any kind of bad behavior while on a group walk, the more second nature it becomes and the harder it is to change later.

Just as for any group training, you must spend some time teaching behaviors individually to each dog before you combine them. Walking in a group is probably the group activity in which this is the most important. When I first started walking more than one

LILIAN WALKING TITAN, JJ AND PHOENIX. TITAN IS WEARING A GENTLE LEADER® TO ASSIST WITH MANAGEMENT AND PHOENIX CARRIES HIS OWN MANAGEMENT DEVICE (A BALL) IN HIS MOUTH.

dog at a time (or actually more than two), I made sure they were all walking well on loose leash one-on-one with me first. But that fact alone did not ensure that they would walk on loose leash when we all walked together.

I used management tools at first, such as a head halter. I also tried every no pull harness that was on the market at the time and can honestly say that none of them worked until the front clip harnesses came out. Once I discovered those, I began using them for all of the dogs, but I quickly determined that two of my dogs were just fine with just their Martingale collars, and Siri only needed a management device until she was trained to focus better. She has long since graduated to just her Martingale. Merlin wore a head halter at first, but some dogs just don't care that something is confining their face and they twist and turn anyway; those are the dogs who are not good candidates for that tool. For him, I simply concentrated on consistency in not moving forward with tension on the leash. He was my biggest loose leash walking challenge. There were many days on our favorite wooded trails where I stood still for a good five minutes at minimum waiting for Merlin to remember that I was there. That time was well spent. Kera briefly wore a head halter but it became clear very quickly that Kera is a near perfect angel (except in the car!) who rarely does anything inappropriate on walks.

Experimenting with various management tools to use on group walks will help to get the process rolling along more smoothly. But let me say something very important about management tools: I am NOT in favor of any sort of tools, whether for management or training, that cause pain or were specifically designed to cause pain when the dog does not comply. Some tools that fall into this category are choke chains, pinch or prong collars or shock collars of any kind. Do not resort to using these tools. Your dogs deserve better. It is far better to spend the time necessary to train the behavior that you want from your dogs, rather than relying on pain causing tools to suppress bad behaviors or to try and make things easier on yourself. Punishment-based tools can often create worse behaviors than you were trying to change.

Choke chains can cause trachea damage and most dogs will still pull with them on anyway. Choke chains (often called training collars or slip collars) give you no leverage at all as far as helping you to stay upright. The prong or pinch collar can cause a little or a

The fastest way to compromise the trust between you and all of your crew members is to use management tools that are designed to cause pain. You will then be seen as unpredictable. Your crew will not fully understand why they are being subjected to the pain that devices such as choke chains, prong collars or shock collars can cause. Much of the time, they will associate this pain with something other than what you intended to teach them. It can often become even harder to fix the behavior that you were trying to adjust, once you venture into the world of punitive training devices. It is far safer all around, not to mention easier, to simply focus on scientifically proven and dog friendly positive behavior modification.

lot of pain depending on how it is used. This may cause your dog to associate the pain that he felt with whatever he was looking at at the time that the pain occurred. Add to that a potential loss of trust between you and your dog, and you have lost more than you have gained. And many dogs still pull with them on; they learn how to pull into the collar to minimize the pain, so you don't get the desired result.

How do I know this? I am what is known in this industry as a crossover trainer. I did use choke chains and prong collars at one time and I will never be able to forget that I subjected my dogs to them. I will also never forget the cry that Siri made when the prong collar hurt her. That was the last time I used that tool. It now holds my back gate closed when the wood is swollen. And the shock collar is something I cannot say anything good at all about. This book would be far longer if I started sharing my thoughts on that, but instead, I'll recommend that you visit the Truly Dog Friendly website and read the wealth of information available there.

Here's how other people handle their multiple dog management.

Real Life Group Walks

JOYCE HAS HAD UP TO FOUR DOGS at once and currently has three. When she had four, the two best-behaved were attached to her homemade waist leash (a sturdy belt with the leashes looped through it). And she held the leashes of the other two. Now that she has three dogs, Jessie is attached to the waist leash and Kendra's and Baxter's leashes are still hand held. *She makes sure that they all have a very reliable "wait", "let's go", "come", "this way" and "leave it" before they are added to the group walk.*

CHRIS HAS A NEWBORN DAUGHTER *and manages to walk three dogs with the stroller. Chris has had more than three dogs at a time, so only three is a breeze! She uses a connector to connect all the leashes together and off they go.*

JEN USUALLY ONLY WALKS TWO OF HER FOUR DOGS *together at this time, as one is a youngster and not as calm as he will be one day and one is new to the home and needs more training. So she and Jeff share walking duties, with Jeff handling Takoda and Jasmine and Jen handling Oskar and Ruby.*

CHERI SOMETIMES WALKS HER CURRENT THREE *all together but according to her, they could use more training as the boys tend to nip at one another as boys of many species are prone to do. Her dog Delanie, however, walks like a perfect lady—unless of course, there is an unknown dog or cat in the vicinity, and then she forgets her manners. Cheri admits they have dragged her on occasion.*

LILIAN WALKS ALL THREE *of her large dogs together. If she is going on a long walk, she'll wear a waist leash and each dog will be attached to her waist leash and a fifteen foot line. For neighborhood walks, Titan wears a head halter and the rest are walked on their Martingales. She tries to keep Titan on the left, Phoenix in the middle and JJ on the side. JJ loves to change sides and walk behind her. She admits that if he were trained to stay in front of her, her walks would go smoother!*

SUSAN SOMETIMES WALKS TWO OF HER DOGS *at once, but more typically, she walks them one at a time in order to spend one-on-one time with them.*

THE BATES CREW WORKING THEIR MUSCLES AND HEARTS.

Exercise and the Multiple Dog Household

I have mentioned some of this already in a previous chapter but I cannot repeat it too much. Hopefully, you already believed in exercising your dog daily before you ventured into the world of multiple dog living. You would be wise to continue that practice now that you have increased the size of your crew. If you were not, I recommend that you very seriously consider it. Having a fenced yard does not mean that you do not need to exercise your dogs. Simply playing in the yard, even with playmates, both canine and human, does not give most dogs enough exercise, especially in a multiple dog household. The value of the proper amount of exercise cannot be overstated. This is another one of those foundations that you will use to build a strong base for your crew.

Exercise goes right along with nutrition in creating a calmer base behavior so that you have fewer issues to start with. However, you need not spend all day exercising your dogs. Even the fittest people on the planet don't do that, so don't set your bar that high. Aim for thirty to sixty minutes most days each week, longer if you can and every day for best results. Bad weather should not deter you. And if you have the opportunity, go for longer walks on weekends. Your dogs and your own health will benefit. Your weekday walks can be broken into two shorter sessions if need be, or one longer one when you get home from work, if you work a standard workweek schedule.

All dogs benefit from exercise. Even older dogs need regular lung filling exercise. I have two dogs that turned eleven years old at the time of this writing. They do the same length walk as the eight- and five-year-old. The only difference between their exercise programs is that the youngest runs around more when off leash, but in colder weather, they all run around a great deal! Exercise itself is only one of the reasons for walking or even running your dogs outside of your yard.

Don't forget about the smells! They need to check their pee mail. Smelling the scents outside of their regular area can occupy a dog's mind far longer than simply the length of the walk. It will go a long way towards alleviating any boredom, adding the environmental stimulation they need in order to be a calm and peaceful crew. Think about how you feel when you go places out of your ordinary routine. Satisfied, a bit or more tired, depending on where you went, usually happier, hopefully! This is what you will be doing for your crew. Of course, that does not mean you don't need to play with your dogs if you walk them. Don't stop playing, playing is good! But walks are important. Walks are meat, playing is dessert.

> Regular exercise will help your multiple dog household run much more smoothly. Regular interactive play is equally important. They both stimulate your dog's minds and bodies. Exercise that takes place outside of the home area is very important. Variety is the spice of life. Being exposed to a variety of sights and smells on a regular basis helps to stimulate your dog's mind. This creates a calmer and happier dog. It is equally important in bad weather as it is in good weather.

Pay attention to each dog. If you have one dog with health issues that make longer walks painful or difficult, then just take that dog on short walks. If any walk, long or short, is an issue with a certain dog, then find a way to get him out of his regular area for a change of surroundings; this will help his emotional state. Try your best to get all of your dogs on a regular outdoor exercise program. If you are the one that has walking difficulties, then enlist a willing friend or neighbor or hire a dog walker to come a few days a week if that is a financial option. If it isn't, don't give up. Think of ways you can possibly trade services, especially if you have very friendly dogs and a neighborhood child who has a strong interest in animals.

I walk my own dogs in all weather except hard downpours. We walk in regular rain, though we do try very hard to go when the rain is lightest, obviously, and according to my schedule availability. We walk in snow and we think snowstorms are great fun. If you have short haired dogs, get coats and maybe boots, depending on how much salt lines your snow covered streets. If we are having a torrential downpour day and can't walk at all (which is really rare), then I take them all up into my finished attic which is big enough for everyone to run around and roughhouse. I run around with them and let them wrestle and play for about an hour, until they are panting and happy. They sometimes play up there even when we do walk. I have a fairly large fenced yard for the city so as you can see, my dogs get quite a bit of exercise and they would take more. If you are looking for an exercise program to get into shape, look no further. Multiple dog ownership is it!

Transporting the Crew

While some of you may simply walk out of your front door and down the street to get your dogs to their exercise spot, many others like me will have to drive the crew to the park or other outdoor places for exercise. Hopefully, you also take them to other fun-filled places in the car so that they are well-socialized and environmentally stimulated. So how does that car ride go with multiple dogs? Most people who have multiple dogs have larger vehicles. I know I do! Although it is not the "greenest" option or the least expensive it certainly is the handiest option when you have a large crew, particularly when you have a multiple human household as well.

> Restrict movement with safety devices as needed, especially for longer trips. With dogs who are more adventurous in the car, always restrict movement.

To crate or not to crate? Well, there are pros and cons for both. Personally, I don't crate for traveling but that doesn't mean you shouldn't. It all depends on

MERLIN, SIRI, KERA AND TRENT AFTER A WALK. THIS IS MY WAY OF TRANSPORTING MY CREW VERY SHORT DISTANCES, SUCH AS TO THE PARK A HALF MILE A WAY. LONGER TRANSPORTS REQUIRE MORE THAN THIS TO BE SAFE.

your own situation. My own dogs travel well together. No one gets snarky with another and that allows me to let them travel mostly loose in my vehicle. However, they are only truly loose if we travel locally. And honestly, I should seatbelt them for anything outside of the half mile away park trips. You cannot control other people's driving and what if someone hits your car and a door is opened? Your dogs could be loose in traffic and get badly hurt. They could also become airborne inside your vehicle and not only could they be harmed by that, the humans inside can be harmed by them. I see many people driving with small dogs on their laps. That is such a bad idea for everyone, both inside the vehicle and out. Please travel with your multiple dogs responsibly.

For your dogs' (and the human's) safety, you have two primary options. Doggy seatbelts are a great way to keep your dog safe and secure, and there are many doggy seat belts on the market. My personal preference is the Ruff Rider Roadie. My dogs wear seatbelts on longer trips. I strongly recommend that you do not leash your dogs to anything in your vehicle by their necks. Seatbelts are usually (or should be) harness based so that if there is a crash of any kind, their necks will not be injured. If you use front clip harnesses on your dogs to walk them, you can always use this as a makeshift seatbelt. Carabineers are handy things to keep in your vehicle, especially if you have an SUV. SUV's usually have several places in their interiors that contain straps that carabineers and leashes can be attached to.

The other option is crating. Crating is safer for your dog in the case of an accident. It is definitely a good option if your dogs have spatial issues and travel badly together. Many SUV's and vans can handle multiple crates, especially if you have smaller dogs. It is also certainly permissible to crate one or two dogs and have the other dogs either loose (for short trips) or secured by a seat belt. This is another case of the "life is not fair" thing. If the dog who has the spatial issues is crated, that sends a message to that dog. If you wish, you can gradually train that dog to travel in a seatbelt instead. But if there is any chance that you might have a fight while you are driving, it is IMPERATIVE that you find a way to safely transport your crew. Driving is hard enough without having to worry about fighting dogs at the same time!

Chapter 7

Choreographing the Crew
Group Training

Among your crew, you may have one or two who respond to certain requests from you better than the others. It will always be that way in some respects. Just like people, dogs all have unique personalities and quirks so some will be a little sharper or more compliant than others. But training your crew will make the compliance differences smaller. How can you accomplish this? Well, it's simple, First you train each one separately and then you add one dog and then another dog and so on and then you train them as a group. You will need to separate them in order to train them individually, but if possible, try to let them watch each other train. My dogs watch each other train when we train at home. At other times, I take one dog to a class or an event with me for some one-on-one time. Everyone gets training; some dogs get more training than others, depending on what the issue is.

Among my crew of four, three of my dogs are fully trained to behave appropriately in most situations and one is still a work-in-progress for some outdoor situations. That dog, Trent, gets more one-on-one training than the other three, but they all get a decent amount of training attention. However, I tend to incorporate quite a bit of training into daily life rather than set specific training time aside. But we do that, too, as needed. Training is fun for them and keeps their minds engaged. Training never stops, even when your dogs have

> Every interaction that you have with your crew trains them in some way. The sooner that you ensure that you are teaching them things you want them to utilize in the future, the better for everyone.

reached the point that they can behave reasonably well in public and at home. Every interaction that you have with your dogs is teaching them something. The sooner you make it a positive something that becomes a part of every day life, the better. It's easier to interact appropriately on a daily basis than it is to fix inappropriate interaction at a later date.

That said, let's mention again something I brought up in an earlier chapter: life is not always fair. Your dogs need to understand this sooner rather than later, as it will help to prevent behavior issues on many levels. Does this mean that some dogs get more of something than others? It can sometimes seem that way if you practice dog sports, competitive obedience, etc. with one dog and not others. However, in those instances, I suggest that you simply have other activities that you do with the other dogs on a regular basis to help offset that imbalance. Even playing with a special toys counts here!

Extra time with just one dog is not the only thing I am referring to when I say that life isn't fair. Preventing your other dogs from being resentful of that time is part of it though. It's all about balance. Maybe you take one dog to agility every week. Maybe you take another on a solo walk. And with yet another, you regularly play a special game he likes. You get the idea.

> Your dogs need to have a grasp that life is not always fair. There will always be occasions where one dog gets something another dog doesn't, such as a class, a vet trip, etc. Strive to balance these instances properly so that everyone gets special time in some way. When your dogs feel comfortable that all their needs are regularly met, instances such as this go much more smoothly. A matter of fact attitude helps these times seem normal, as they should be.

Your dogs should feel comfortable that they are taken care of and that their needs are met so when you leave for a show with one dog, the others take it in stride. They know they will get their time another day in another way. It also helps to be matter of fact when you need to give one or two dogs something that the others don't get. It's up to you to do that in such a way and frequently enough that it's not a shock or a resource issue. Life isn't fair extras can include extra pets, kisses, walks, pills, special treats that hide pills, extra attention because of a medical issue, a solo dog trip to a class, etc. The possibilities are endless but just be aware that the whole *life isn't always fair* idea needs to be taught early on so that the potential problems are drastically reduced.

Avoid placing too much emphasis on whatever extra you give to one dog. Being very matter of fact is important to pulling this off properly. Feeling guilty about giving one dog something extra will make it more notable. Dogs will catch onto that. As mentioned in a previous chapter, continually favoring one dog over others WILL cause problems. Varying who gets something extra because of varying needs and situations is a whole different scenario, however. Strive for balance. While something may not be fair at that moment, things will balance out at another time. That's up to you to convey to your dogs. Benevolent leadership (explained in Proofing the Pups) will greatly help this process.

Now back to training a group. When I set time aside to train my dogs, I use a baby gate to block my kitchen off. Three of the dogs are on one side of the gate and I have one dog with me. We use that time to train whatever behaviors that dog needs or for fun stuff like tricks. The requirements will vary with each dog so this is a good opportunity to start the *"life is not always fair"* lesson. However, in this case, everyone gets a turn. My dogs are very excited to watch each other train and it fuels their desire to have their turn, in a good way. There is no jostling for the next position. They act appropriately

TRENT, SIRI & KERA WAITING FOR THEIR TURN TO TRAIN.

when the gate is opened for the next dog. This makes for an eager-to-learn dog.

You can and should vary the order in which they get to train. But one caveat: if you have a dog who is much pushier or quick to take a mile when you give him an inch, then that dog should go last until his impulse control and pushiness improves. If that behavior varies with the day, then whoever is most patient goes first and so on. Reward appropriate behavior and it gets better from there!

> Vary the rewards that you use when training. Of course, treats should be number one on your list but make sure that you vary among the types of treats within any given training session. But don't stop there. Toys, petting, tug, hugs, etc. Make a list of everything each dog considers a reward and use all that apply when training them.

Start your training sessions by working on the skills your dog most needs in a group situation, such as fast name recognition, a "wait", "sit", "down", an attention cue (look at me), "come", "leave it" and anything else you can think of. Don't forget to throw some tricks in as well, here and there. Those will definitely vary per dog. These daily life necessity cues should all be pretty solid before you add another dog to the training session. The length of the session that you have with each dog is up to you but making it short and leaving him wanting more is a great way to keep a dog eager to train whenever you have time for it.

> Training a multiple dog household starts with training each dog individually. They should watch each other train when possible. Dogs can learn by watching other dogs do tasks, especially when the reward is food!

And make time you should. I won't lie to you: training all of your dogs to be well trained as a group is not something you can do in a day or two. It takes patience and diligence. But it is very rewarding! As far as step-by-step instructions for each of these cues, I have provided some basic instructions in Proofing the Pups, but I do suggest that you learn all you can and review the books in the reference section. Several that I have recommended can be of assistance to any multiple dog home.

I highly recommend using a release cue to let the dog or dogs know when you are done with each cue. This will be useful whether you are training one dog at a time or all of them together. You will also use the release cue when your training session is complete. Used successfully, this release cue has myriad uses from "done training" to "no more people food treats." Yes, I have a cue for that after dinner and it's very handy. When choosing a release cue, many people use "okay" to release their dogs. I am not a big fan of using "okay" as a release cue. Why? Because that word is used so much throughout a day in normal conversation, it's common place to our dogs as well. In addition, if you place your dogs in a stationary cue outside and someone walks within hearing distance and says, "okay", they have released your dogs! Just say no to "okay.".

> Utilizing a release cue to let your dogs know when you are done with an exercise is important so the crew is not left to their own decision making processes on this subject!

I use "free!" as a release cue. You can make up your own. Use whatever you want. Just make sure that it's not a word that you already use frequently in another context. Common release cues are "all done", "go play", "go", and even "release". Be creative! One caution on this: I have had some clients use the cue "come" for a release cue and then also use it to mean "come to me right now". I strongly urge you not to use these cues interchangeably. Any word that you use to mean "come to me right now" is not the cue that should be used to release your dog from a stationary cue. Stationary cues should mean to retain the position you cued your dog into, until you come back and release him. This ensures that there is never a reason for your dog to think that sometimes you call him out of such a cue. If your dog learns that he always stays in said cued place until you return, the cue is much more solid than if he is sometimes called out of the cue.

A word regarding baby gates: baby gates are a great way to conduct one-on-one training while the rest wait for a turn. This won't work for everyone as some dogs are simply going to be too exuberant to wait behind a baby gate. You will know if you have one! If this sounds like one of your crew, then you may need to either tether or crate him while you train the others, at least at first. I strongly believe that training like this is far more effective; when the crew is able to watch each other train, it benefits everyone. If you can, either tether or crate even the most lively dog in the same room as the other dogs so you can train each dog within view of the other dogs.

What if you have a barker? Well, that simply means you must be a bit more creative. Training under these conditions will teach you much patience. Here's a great tip. You can use the group mentality in your favor. Tune out the barker and increase the verbal rewards with the dog or dogs you are training at the moment. If the results of your little screamer's efforts are more attention for another dog, he learns pretty quickly to watch quietly! The only time your strong-lunged little darling will get acknowledged is when he is quiet. It's very important in this situation that you do not acknowledge the barking in any way. Negative attention is still attention.

> Having an attention seeking barker among your crew creates a special challenge. This dog will be easier than you think to train but you will need extra patience and precise timing. It is more important for you to reward NOT barking than for you to pay any attention at all to the barking.

Weaning the barker out of the crate for this exercise will happen in steps. You will learn to use this kind of competition with any situation where it may be needed. But you will need to be careful so as not to create a whole new set of problems. We discuss more about competition in other chapters as well.

So now you have carefully trained each dog to behave as you wish individually. Are you ready to put them together and see how it goes? Well, depending on how well your dogs have learned things so far and how many dogs you have, you have several options. In general, I think it's best to add one dog at a time. So take your most responsive dog and add the next most responsive and lower your criteria a bit. What I mean by lowering the criteria is simply this: don't make the requests as hard as you would have with just one dog being trained. Why? Well, you have just changed the rules and now you cannot expect the same compliance with an added

Raising, lowering and changing criteria: this is a very fluid principle. If you have your dog trained to do something in a certain situation and you try using the same cue in a different situation, you have changed the criteria. When you change the criteria, you should make it easier to comply in order to set your dog up for success. For example, your dog knows how to come to you 100% successfully in the house. When you take this cue outside, you do this in steps. Perhaps the next step is in your secluded fenced in yard when you are standing only a few feet away. You are now lowering the criteria to ensure success. Once this has been successfully mastered, you might stand a few more feet away. You would then be raising the criteria. You might raise or lower criteria many times within any given time frame. Know your dog's signals and never ask for too much. The training will be much more solid if you do this at your dog's speed.

distraction (in this case, another dog).

This is another basic principle of training that is helpful in training any dog, but especially in a multiple dog home. Additional information on this and other training principles will be in the chapter, Proofing the Pups. Reading some of the books suggested in the Resources section will also help you understand more fully. To sum this up, any time you add something new, you make your requests a bit easier than those you just successfully completed.

Do this step with each dog. Mix up the dogs, then add a dog to the training session until you have them all together successfully. That's where the real fun begins. You can make competition healthy and fun. Leave the cutthroat behind by making sure that everyone's impulse control is pretty good before you do this in a group. You can reward whoever sits fastest when you issue a group sit. So how do you issue a group sit? Well, start by asking each dog by name to sit. Reward that. Then decide on a name for your group cueing. I

Create a group cue that you will use to mean all of your dogs should do something you ask. Many dogs learn faster by watching other dogs successfully do something. This will be helpful when teaching a group cue.

SAMMY, GEORGE, SALLY, DOVER AND TOBY DOING A HAPPY GROUP STAY.

use "puppies". As in "puppies sit", "puppies watch". I make it all one big cue. You can use whatever you want, but make it consistent. It's important for your dogs to grasp that this means all of them.

That is why I suggest that when you first get them all together in a group for training, ask each dog by name to do something. Reward each dog for complying and then try the group cue. Reward compliance. Make a show of verbally rewarding the fastest to comply, but do still reward all dogs who comply, with treats. The first treat should go to the fastest to comply but if one dog is not getting it, then start upping your verbal rewarding while dispensing the treats as well. Make sure that you use a marker such as a clicker or a "yes" and that your dogs fully understand this marker is important to the group compliance.

Most dogs do learn by watching the action, in addition to other learning methods. Seeing everyone else comply with a "sit" and getting marked and rewarded will go a long way towards registering what you want in their amazing little brains. Once they seem to grasp that you mean all of them, start marking and treating all of them as close to one another as possible.

An important note: mix up the treat order if they are all about the same speed. You want the dogs to behave smoothly as a group, so even though you use some competition to train this group cue, you will not continue the competition after they get it, unless a dog or two gets distracted. And that will happen. They are, after all, living beings, not robots, so although training will make things run much more like clockwork than without, there will always be challenges big and small. But with practice, it will become second nature.

When do group cues come in handy? The examples are nearly endless. I use "wait" at the door to the yard, at the gate when leaving to go somewhere in the car, in the car when running errands and leaving them there; "sit" almost anywhere, often combined with other cues; "watch" on walks; "come" in the house as well as at off-leash play sessions. You will have ample opportunity to practice these cues once taught. As in training just one dog, you will need to use rewards a great deal, especially when first training the cues. The most obvious reward will be high value treats, but you know your dogs best so do not discount the value of other rewards such as toys, praise, petting, etc.

Even using the Premack principle can be appropriate here. For example, I use this principle on walks. My dogs like to chase squirrels, as I am sure many of yours do as well. I use a group "watch" and when I get more than a perfunctory compliance, I release them (on leash) to pretend to try and climb the tree with the squirrel and whine for a little bit. They get what they want and I get what I want. It's a win/win situation. If I don't get complete compliance by all of the dogs, then I make a HUGE fuss over the dogs who are paying attention and they get showered with treats. That usually does the trick. You can use these "life rewards" in many situations, both inside and out. I'll discuss more on the walking-related compliance and training "*Taking it on the Road*".

> The Premack principle in a nutshell: use something that a dog wants to do as a reward for doing something that you want your dog to do. The surrounding paragraph contains an example. Here's another: your dog wants to sniff a certain area. Stop and wait patiently until your dog turns around and looks at you, mark the moment (yes!) and then permit your go to the spot he wants to sniff.

In the house, once you have done the appropriate share of individual training, then added dogs one or two at a time and then proofed the training, you can start to experiment. For example, if all of your dogs are in the same room as you but they are not focused on you, take this opportunity to try a group recall. When you first start doing this as a group, don't use a recall cue. Just sound REALLY happy and use whatever endearment words you use with your dogs to get their attention. Reward heavily when they come to you. Use treats on occasion, even if you have to get up and go to the kitchen to get them. You want to make this memorable. Once you have them coming to you in the same room reliably, start using your group cue. (puppies, boys, girls, dogs, etc.) You get the idea.

As your dogs make progress in their training, move slowly. It is better to move along slowly than move too fast before a dog is ready to progress. Set them up for success. Be sure before you move ahead. After they are successfully coming to one cue, then start adding the recall cue after the group cue. One tip when using the recall cue: as in training this cue in the first place, you should be very careful about how you use your recall word. If you have any doubts that they will comply ASAP, then think of a word that you want to mean "start heading in my direction" as opposed to "drop everything and COME RIGHT NOW". You can work with the group on that second, more urgent cue after you master the first one.

If you have not mastered this more urgent cue with your dogs, you should work on that ASAP before you attempt to match this action with a word. If one or more of your dogs do not immediately comply when you use your recall word, despite a lot of time training for this cue, then you will need to think of a new word before you start training them to respond as a group. Once again, you must start training the new cue individually and then as a group. Use the former recall cue as that "start heading in my direction" cue and use a new one for the "drop everything and COME RIGHT NOW" cue.

Training a solid recall cue should be one of your more important endeavors. Make coming to you the best thing that your dogs ever do. This should be the equivalent of doggy party time! If you have accidentally created a reliable recall cue (want a cookie?, etc.) use that as your emergency recall cue. Reward heavily for compliance.

One thing that I have discovered about a recall cue in my years with multiple dogs is that most people inadvertently teach their dogs something that causes them to immediately come running from any corner of the house. Mine turned out to be "who wants a piece?" as in after dinner when I am sharing what I have saved for them. I have heard others such as "cookie", "wanna go for a ride", "dinner", etc. Think about whether you have one. If you do, you now have at your disposal what I call an emergency recall word. You can use this when outside if a dog is not coming when called while off leash or if a dog gets loose. Do not overuse it. It will lose its effectiveness and meaning. Just remember that it's there when you need it, like the fire extinguisher in your kitchen. Emergencies only, okay?

Now back to practicing that group recall. Your next step is to call your dogs when they are not in the room with you. In your happiest voice (the one that sounds like you are going to have the very best dog party ever) loudly call them by their group cue (no recall word yet, since you have changed criteria) and if you hear any of them coming, use your voice to happily encourage them to continue to come. Have your best treats handy and loudly and enthusiastically reward all who come to you. Be sure to reward them all equally if they have arrived at approximately the same time. Dole out the treats and pets and make it fun! Count to fifteen and use every single second of that to have the very best dog party. If you have a straggler, make your acknowledgment of the compliant ones even more enthusiastic, if that is possible.

Typically, using what I call the cheerleader voice will cause all the dogs to want to find out what they are missing. So if you do have a straggler, be sure you are sounding as happy and encouraging as you think you are. I always say that if you are embarrassed by the way you sound, you are doing it correctly. About that straggler: once he reaches you, be sure to verbally reward him. But it is okay to make it a bit lower key than for the rest. When your dogs are once again relaxed, quietly leave the room (if you use a "wait" cue, now would be a great time to use it) and once you are in the other room, repeat what you just did. After a few times practicing this, start adding the recall cue after the group cue, just as they are headed towards you.

Every time you change the criteria (change rooms, add distance, make it harder in some way) back off on using the recall word and go back to just the group cue. Give better treats for the faster responder. You can use healthy competition in this scenario. However, do not reward or condone any rude pushing and shoving. Any rudeness gets the offender rewarded last, quietly, once the rudeness has abated. To not reward is to not reward the recall and you must acknowledge the appropriate behavior. I very verbally reward those who act appropriately and give them more treats. If pushing and shoving gets an offender less rewards for them and more for the others, they quickly learn to act appropriately.

Body language goes a long way towards getting this point across. While I only verbally acknowledge the bad behavior in a group if it needs to be interrupted immediately, I do use my body language to say things in other ways. Examples of this can include turning away from the rude dog and blocking him from being a part of the group that I am addressing. This technique is usually effective in getting my point across when the effusive verbal rewarding of the others doesn't. Conduct group practice daily, moving around various parts of the house and slowly adding criteria and difficulty. Once you have this down pat in the house in many areas with the recall cue, and then take it in the yard. If you don't have fencing, then go to a secure area outside, such as a tennis court or an empty dog park or anyplace you have locally on a time and day with few distractions. You can never practice a recall too much.

I highly recommend taking positive reinforcement training classes as well, in order to get hands-on, in-person assistance in learning how to deal with any situation. I have mentioned this in several sections of this book; I cannot repeat it enough. There is no such thing as too much training. In addition to helping to forge a strong bond between you and each dog individually, classes will help your dogs focus on you in the midst of distractions. See the resources section for assistance in how to choose a positive trainer.

If you have a dog or two with strong reactivity issues but you feel that you can modify the behavior in a class setting, then look for classes specific to this subject as well. These classes often have names such as "Feisty Fidos" or "Rowdy Rovers", or simply have the word reactive in the title of the class. See the resources section as well for book suggestions on this subject. But please do not stop at a book if the behavior that your dog is exhibiting makes you feel that he may be a danger to anything, human or animal. Get professional assistance ASAP. It will be well worth it. Another type of class to keep an eye out for is one specifically designed for outdoor distractions. These are also often called "Real Life" classes.

Any positive reinforcement training class that you take your dog to can do several things for both of you. Classes can help you strengthen the bond between you and each dog that you attend with. The class will also help to socialize each dog for new situations. I take turns taking my dogs to various dog social events as well as classes. Doing these things not only gives you one-on-one time with each dog: it helps each dog to learn to that there is more than being a part of a crew. Teaching each dog to be comfortable with and without his crew is important. It creates a more confident dog.

Real Life Group Training

WHEN LILIAN WORKS WITH HER DOGS *individually, depending on the weather, she takes them one by one onto the porch, into the back-yard or to her finished basement. The others are usually besides themselves and whining for their turn. Lilian actually prefers to practice her group training in real life situations.*

CRYSTAL TENDS TOWARDS GROUP TRAINING *sessions with her large crew, including foster dogs as well.*

SUSAN TRAINS HER CREW *both one-on-one and in a group, depending on what she needs to work on. She uses her fenced yard for group sessions. She also takes advantage of real life situations such as visitors arriving to use group cues such as sit and stay.*

Chapter 8

Play by Play
Kids Just Wanna Have Fun

Dog play: important or frivolous? Some people might think that giving dogs the opportunity to play is unimportant. But play is very important for a dog's wellbeing. Dogs need a play outlet just as humans do. At the very minimum, playing helps to release tension and relieve stress. A dog who gets to play regularly is a happier, healthier dog. But when you have multiple dogs, you need to be observant during play.

If you are currently having no issues with playtime in your multiple dog home, then keep doing what you are doing. Most dogs who have lived together on a regular basis will likely play well together with little or no supervision. But keep in the back of your mind that changes in circumstances, no matter how small, can sometimes change dynamics in the household. Often these changes will manifest themselves in a play session. This is especially true when you add a new dog to your crew.

When human visitors are present, your crew will be more playful. There will also be more of a chance for a skirmish since excitement is at a higher level. Play behavior that would usually be okay when only the family is present can quickly turn into a fight. Break up play frequently when you have such a scenario. Being in charge of play keeps it controllable.

Unless you are having problems between certain dogs in another area of behavior, typically you won't have issues during play without a human around. An audience presence always ups the ante and creates a higher excitement element. This is especially true when your dogs play when human guests are present. Be aware of this potential.

I tend to break up the play periodically to keep the excitement level manageable. I do this when it's just my own dogs but especially when there are human and/or canine guests present. It really helps your dogs to remember that you are there.

> Permitting your dogs to play too much can have the opposite effect from what you intended. They will remain in a constant state of high excitement which will make it harder for them to relax. Balance play with calm down time and you will have a dog with better emotional stability.

Briefly practicing some of the cues that your dogs know can refocus them if play gets to an extreme excitement level. Once you get them refocused, you can simply let them go back to playing. If you have younger dogs, they seem to never tire of wrestling and playing. This can promote a constant state of high adrenaline. Even though constant play might seem like a good idea for tiring out your adolescent dogs, it's actually the opposite. When your dog's cortisol levels stay high, he doesn't return to a normal state of calm. The

PENNY, TOBY, AND SALLY PLAYING ROUGH. IT LOOKS SCARY BUT IT'S NOTHING MORE THAN FUN AND GAMES.

TOBY AND GEORGE TAKE A PLAY BREAK.

THE BRAY CREW JUST APPEAR TO BE TORTURING THE PUPPY. IN REALITY, THE PUPPY IS ENJOYING HIS FAUX WRESTLING MATCH.

longer his cortisol level stays high, the harder it is for him to regain a state of calm.

This is why you see an increased reactivity in a dog who has recently been subject to a very high-excitement situation. His mind and body have not recovered fully and he is primed for another excitement incident. This can create a hare trigger reactivity scenario.

It's better to take frequent breaks and have the dogs practice calm between play. This also teaches them to shut play off when need be. You can tether them between play sessions at first if they are not ready to retain a down when you want them to. Tether and reward calm. The reward for appropriate calm can be a return to play.

You may have several different breeds among your crew, with several different play styles. Get familiar with the different play styles of your dogs' breeds so you can more easily tell what is and isn't appropriate. I have both herding and guarding/working breeds with a splash of northern breed thrown in to keep it interesting. Two of my dogs have a very physical body-bashing play style with a lot of front paw usage and the other two have more of a herding breed play style, which includes a lot of barking and chasing, poking/pinching and leg grabbing. They play fine with one another and have almost combined the two styles among themselves. This can happen with dogs that are very close to one another and this is a good thing.

AN EXAMPLE OF PACK BEHAVIOR THAT MIGHT ESCALATE WHEN YOUR DOGS ARE EN MASSE AMONG OTHER DOGS THEY DON'T KNOW.

When your dogs can understand each other's play signals, that is a sign of a well mixed crew. Be grateful for this if you attain it.

As noted in a previous chapter, it would be very helpful to any multiple dog home to become familiar with body language. There are DVD's and books that you can watch and read in order to learn what the dogs are saying with their bodies and facial expressions. Please refer to the *Resources* section for suggestions. What you think you are interpreting from observing the play may not be

Isis (left) and Rocky play sparring style while Cinder "directs" from the sideline. This kind of combative playstyle is common with working breeds and can look scary. As long as you know what is actually play, then this is fun for your dogs.

Merlin and Siri are pretending to be bossy while Trent is pretending to submit to them. This is a confrontational style play common within the working breeds."

KEEMA TRYING TO ENTICE ZEKE INTO PLAY WHILE NIKKO TRIES TO INTERVENE. RAVEN WATCHES THE ACTION WHILE NICOLAI IGNORES IT.

ZOLA AND SKYLER PLAY GROWLY FACE AT THE BEACH. THIS CAN LOOK SCARY BUT THIS IS A VERY COMMON PLAYSTYLE WITH WORKING BREEDS

PENNY, TOBY, SALLY AND BRANDI (L-R CLOCKWISE) CHASE EACH OTHER WHILE GEORGE PATROLS THE PERIMETER. CHASING STYLE PLAY IS COMMON WITH MANY BREEDS, ESPECIALLY HERDING AND HUNTING BREEDS."

A SPORTING BREED (WITH A TOKEN BORDER COLLIE MIX) ROMP IN THE SNOW CAN BE ROUGH AND TUMBLE. MANY DOGS CAN GET FRISKIER WHEN PLAYING IN SNOW.

KIRA SHOWING KEEMA WHAT LOOKS TO BE A VERY THREATENING FACE, A NORMAL PLAY STYLE FOR SIBERIAN HUSKIES AND OTHER WORKING BREEDS."

Mia and Zeke are ganging up on Nikko (who is enjoying it!) while Jenna cheers them on."

Mia and Nicolai having a chew on Nikko in the pool. Many breeds don't like to play in water. It's actually unsual for Sibes to do this. But having water available for summertime play can be very helpful to your crew regardless of their breeds."

Become familiar with the different play styles of the breeds that you have among your crew. It is important that you recognize what is and isn't okay when you see it. This is especially important if you plan to frequent dog parks with your crew. If you have a crew full of confident dogs, the dog park at peak usage time might not be the best place for your dogs to fulfill their play quota. Be honest with yourself regarding your crew's potential for bullying other dogs to avoid problems at the dog park.

accurate. Some dogs can appear to be aggressive when they are simply playing. A good example of that is in the picture of Toby with his teeth bared and Sally with her mouth on Toby's ear. The opposite can also be true. Some dogs' negative reactivity is so subtle that you may miss it until they strike and then you have a fight on your hands. Learning what to watch for will help you maintain control and prevent fights.

A word about dog parks: I am not a fan of taking all dogs from a multiple dog home to a dog park all at once unless you are going when no one else is there. Dog parks do have the advantage of offering a larger leash-free area than most people have at home for running within the safe confines of fencing. Yet when other dogs are at the dog park, introducing your whole crew into the situation can cause a problem. When you have several members of a multiple dog home all together, they have a tendency to act like a pack. They may be individual dogs in your mind, but among other canines who may be there alone or perhaps with one other dog, your multiple dog crew has back up. They will feel far more confident in this situation than is necessarily desirable.

If you insist on going to a dog park when there are other dogs present, then don't take your entire crew all at once. Take one or two dogs at a time. As you may have guessed, I am not really a fan of dog parks at all. While they can offer some dogs the opportunity to socialize and exercise, they can also be populated by dog owners who are unfamiliar with appropriate dog behavior, or worse, who are not even bothering to supervise their dogs. Make sure that if you do take your dog(s) to a dog park, that you supervise their play and watch for tell-tale signs of trouble.

KIRA, KEEMA, AND NANOOK ENJOY SOME INDOOR PLAYTIME.

Where you permit your dogs to play in your home is up to you. How you make your decision should in some part depend upon how they play.

If you do not permit play inside your home and you do not have a fenced yard, it is really important that you make sure to provide a place for your dogs to play on a regular basis. The aforementioned dog parks at off-hours are an option. But when you have your crew at such a place en masse, choose a time when you're certain no one else will be there.

If your dogs have doggy friends, and they should, then maybe one of those doggy friends has a fenced yard to play in. I often take my dogs to a nearby dog-friendly cemetery near my home to walk. After the walk, if no one is around, I allow them to run and play off-leash in a specific area that I can control comfortably. My dogs are very well

> Provide a regular play outlet for your crew in a safe venue. If you do not possess a fenced in yard and if you prefer that your crew not play rough in your home, be vigilant about finding an appropriate place for your dogs to play. Operate within the confines of your crew's training. On leash play is fine as long as it's supervised.

NICOLAI, STARBUCK, AND NIKKO HAVE LEASHED PLAYTIME IN THE SNOW.

recall trained. If you have such a spot available to you, do this responsibly. That means being aware of the limits of your dog's training and not permitting them to run rampant, especially if others are around. I come across people all the time who have untrained off-leash dogs running up to other leashed dogs. That isn't polite and can cause a dog fight. Be a responsible multiple dog owner and exercise your dogs appropriately within the limits of what their training safely permits.

If your home is not on a dangerous heavily-traveled street and your dogs are perimeter trained, then off-leash supervised play in your yard is not a bad thing. If this is your solution to play, keep in mind that your dogs should al-

Playing with your dogs is good for you and them! It promotes bonding and increases your connection with your crew. Appropriate play between canine and humans is important. Be aware of the games than can cause any of your crew members to escalate into too high of an excitement level. Use appropriate judgment with games involving tugging, rough housing and you running.

ready be trained to stay within the confines of your yard. Human supervision IS important here as playtime creates a whole different dynamic as far as distractions go. What your dogs know any other time may not always apply while deep in play. This especially applies when you have a group mentality at work. The best defense against your dog's forgetting about you in a high excitement level is that trust thing we have discussed many times. The better the relationship that you develop with your dogs one-on-one and as a group, then the better they will hear you even when they are otherwise occupied. All good things come from you, remember that!

When you add a new canine crew member, supervision is vitally important. I think it's appropriate to let dogs play together with leashes on when you have a new addition. This is supervised play only, of course. Whether all of your dogs need a leash for this situation will depend on each dog's individual personality, so knowing each dog's temperament is important.

Should YOU play with your dogs? Of course!! It's a great bonding opportunity. How you play will depend on your own activity level. Your participation can include throwing a ball, playing tug, and running back and forth with your dog as well as multiple other options. Playing with your dogs is great mental stimulation as well as physical exercise. Enjoy this time with your dogs, but play with rules so that chaos isn't the winner.

JASMINE, OSKAR AND TAKODA PLAYING IN AN UNFENCED YARD. JASMINE IS LEASHED BECAUSE HER TRAINING IS NOT YET COMPLETED.

If you have any compliance issues at all, do not wrestle with your dog(s). If you play tug (and it's a really helpful game to play!) then play with YOU almost always winning when you want the game to end. Do not tolerate any teeth-on-skin during play (or anytime for that matter!) If during play, a dog's teeth touch your skin, play ends. Don't allow your dog to chase you too much, especially if they have herding breed parentage, as this can easily get out of hand. And as noted earlier, be sure to break up play periodically to keep the excitement level manageable.

Chapter 9

Tails are Tucked

Signs the Bloom is Off

You finally have the multiple dog mix you have decided is perfect but something is off. You feel an undercurrent of tension and you cannot quite put your finger on why you think something is up. We shall now discuss signs that you need an intervention of some sort to prevent a worsening of the problem.

Since your dogs can't talk, you will need to learn to read their body language. Their bodies can tell you so much via positioning, mannerisms, facial expressions, ear and tail positions, etc. Reading your dogs' body language is important to understanding the dynamic between your dogs. There are several fine books and DVD's available on dog body language. When you commit to having a multiple dog household, it's important that you get familiar with how dogs communicate, both with each other and you. So beg, borrow or buy one of these books so you can speak their language. You will find some recommended selections are listed in the resources section.

> Get familiar with dog body language in general and your dog's body language in particular. Understanding what you are seeing in your dog's behavior can prevent a multitude of problems.

So what clues might mean trouble may be brewing? Some interactions may just be normal behavior among your crew. I recommend keeping track of the behaviors that bother you to help you determine whether to call in a professional. Here are some clues that you need help NOW.

-Your dogs are fighting on a regular basis and you worry when the next fight will be.

-Your dogs are growling, snarking, snapping and lunging at each other frequently.

-You often feel worried about what will happen when certain dogs are together.

-One or more dogs are guarding food or other high value resources from another, to the point where you are afraid for someone's safety.

-One or more of your dogs are showing hard stares and raised lips at each other on a regular basis.

> Do NOT ignore any of the above signals that something is brewing. Get professional help ASAP. Your dogs depend on you to keep them safe. That includes from on another.

The above behaviors indicate a need for immediate attention from a professional. Run, do not walk, to the phone and call a qualified professional to come in and assist with this. It's important to not let this go on too long, lest you have a tragedy happen. Remember, your dogs depend on you for safety. Keep your promise. Check the resources section for sources to find a behavior consultant near you.

Below I have listed further behaviors that also need attention to nip them in the bud. If you are unsure about how to tip the balance back to normal, then consult a professional. Any of these behaviors have the potential to get worse at any moment. Even if the behavior has been somewhat consistent but has just subtly gotten worse, take action if you are no longer comfortable with it.

So unless you ARE a professional, if you see any of these signs, consult a professional for at least one session just to be sure of what you are seeing. You will either find out that everything is okay or you will get some solid assistance with turning things around. Much of your dogs' interactions can be swayed by your behavior, so having an objective professional watching the interaction between you and your dogs can be very enlightening, and can return your household to serenity. Now back to those signs..........

-One or more dogs are being pushy and rude about another dog's resources, such as not permitting them to play.

-One dog repeatedly pushes the others aside for access to your attention.

-One or more dogs cast worried looks at another dog on a regular basis.

-One dog guards you from the others.

-One of your dogs tries to make himself small and unnoticeable in another dog's presence.

-One of your dogs seems to control the movements of one or more of the others.

-One or more dogs appear to be very stiff around each other.

-Playtime gets uncomfortably out of hand and you have repeatedly had to step in to stop the play.

Until you have these things under better control, management is key. You will always be managing your dogs' behavior to some degree of course, but when there is potential for conflict, such management becomes critical. Some examples of management are feeding some dogs separately or only permitting certain dogs to have a privilege or two.

Get a professional opinion on any of the above mentioned signals. While not necessarily urgent, these could quickly become so if they escalate. In both scenarios, use stringent management until the problems are resolved. Leave nothing to chance!

That kind of management can keep the peace while you are adapting their training to improve the group dynamics. Management helps to prevent your dogs from having the opportunity to practice bad behavior.

So let's say you have two dogs giving each other the hairy eyeball and you are worried whether they are headed for a scuffle. Keep them separated for a bit, or at the very minimum, have the stronger-willed one on leash. If you are having guarding issues, then only give high value items to them when they are in separate rooms or while crated or tethered. If you have two dogs who vie for positions on the couch, both dogs must be kept off the couch until the issues are resolved. Management is one of the most important tools you have in a multiple dog home. It's easier to fix things before they get to the scariest point than it is after all heck has broken loose!

What do you do when your management has been lax and an issue presents itself, such as one dog growling and lunging at another? You must address it, even though it has not progressed to physical contact. The next time the behavior may escalate, so intervene as soon as it happens. Do not yell and scream as that can be the human equivalent of barking and growling to our dogs. The resident human showing an aggressive display (such as yelling) is not the best way to redirect an aggressive display from the dogs! Being calm, confident and in charge is the card you want to play here.

> Using good posture and being tall even when you are petite, will garner respect from your crew. Dogs respect confident body language. You can keep the peace more easily by appearing confident and in control even when you are not feeling that way. Contrary to what you may have heard previously, do NOT let your dogs work it out themselves! That is not their job. You are the crew leader.

How can you show that you are in charge without yelling? Good posture is not only good for you; it's good for your dogs. Dogs respect confident silhouettes. Did you ever notice a dog fluffing himself up when he catches sight of another dog? He tries to make himself big. Dogs respect big. Even if you are a small person like I am, standing tall will help convince your dogs that you are she-who-must be-obeyed! Using your body to direct movement of the dogs can also make a big impression. Body blocking and displacement moves such as "moving tall" through your dogs together can often defuse a situation faster than a voice cue can.

When done properly, time outs are another viable option. Placing the offenders in a down-stay until things are calmer is a form of a time out, if you are comfortable with their compliance on down-stays. Don't ask more than your dogs can handle now. This is not the time to ask for cues that have not been fully trained or that you have spent more time repeating than rewarding. Setting your dogs up to succeed, so you can reward them for good behavior is your ultimate aim here, not punishing them and giving them nothing to aspire to. Make it clear that snarking will result in the removal of attention and will not be rewarded. If jealousy for your attention (positive or negative) is at the root of the issue, then you will have made your point.

If you are at all uncomfortable with the feuding dogs staying in the same room together, then by all means, listen to your gut instinct. Your instincts don't lie. Use baby gates and separate rooms to restore harmony for now. Also, if you have any dogs that were not involved in the initial skirmish, but are happy to jump in to show support for one or the other, then make sure that you include those dogs when you show them what is proper behavior. Continue to be "she-who-must-be-obeyed" with all dogs who need it. Safety is important and even if you have small dogs, they can hurt each other as well as give you some small but nasty bites should you be in the wrong place at the wrong time. And if you have larger dogs, this is even more important. Big dogs have big teeth. Big teeth hurt whatever they connect with. Keeping the peace is better for everyone.

If, much to your dismay, you missed a signal and a fight ensues, stay calm. Being prepared for such occurrences is invaluable. Try to keep certain items on hand to safely break up fights. For instance, a product called Spray Shield® or an air horn can often split up brawlers. Some shelters use something called a breakstick. This is a small length of wood that you use to place in the aggressor's mouth in order to loosen the grip from the dog who is being bitten. You must be quick when you do this so that neither dog can reconnect. Quickly direct them to different rooms and concentrate on having a sturdy hold of the one who is more likely to reconnect. Verbally back the other one off in a different direction. If you are close to the door and have a doorbell, try ringing it. If your dogs respond well to recalls, you can try firmly calling one to you. If that succeeds, use body blocks immediately to prevent a continuation of the fight at a different location. If they simply are not hearing you at all, then the Spray Shield® and the air horn can come in handy.

Other possible solutions are spraying/dousing them with water, whether from a pot or a hose (even the one in your kitchen sink). In a pinch a fire extinguisher will work. DO NOT grab their collars and try to pull them apart. Yes, yes, I know this is your first instinct. But let me offer a couple of reasons why this is not the best option. First,

If you have been having even the slightest fight between any of your crew members, you must have things on hand to prepare to break up dog fights should your management fail. Air horns, citronella spray, a breakstick, a fire extinguisher, a hose, etc. It is urgent that you have a plan in place should it be needed. Do not leave this to chance. And first and foremost, get professional assistance ASAP.

your dog could redirect his aggression to you and that is clearly not what you want to occur. Second, your dogs could have good firm holds on one another and you could turn what might have not even progressed into broken skin into a significant skin tear that will need attention from a veterinary professional.

If you must open a dog's jaws without a breakstick, the following procedure is effective but is best used only by someone confident enough to do it without hesitation. This procedure is only useful when only one dog has a hard grip on the other. Grab the skin directly at the back of the neck, just below the skull, between the ears. Grab this firmly and hold on until the jaws release. Then quickly move the dogs to different areas. You must again be prepared for the dog that is released to try and make contact with the dog that has just let go. But hopefully, the recently freed dog will simply be happy to be that way and will go elsewhere of his own accord. Once you have them in their separate corners, be sure to check each dog thoroughly for injuries and treat accordingly.

Be sure to assume the "she-who-must-be-obeyed" voice and posture once you have separated the dogs and you are assured that no one is more hurt than a little Neosporin® would fix. At this point, particularly if this scuffle started as a conflict over resources such as attention, you must ignore your dogs and not give them any attention once you get them safely ensconced in separate areas. And when I say ignore them, I mean completely ignore them for some notable period of time. Act like they do not exist. Do not acknowledge even a whine or a grumble. No chastising, no nothing. If any of the offenders is loose or near you and nudges for a petting, again, ignore them; no absent-minded petting, no attention, period. You want it to be very clear that what just transpired was unacceptable. Dogs hate to be ignored. Your lesson will likely not be lost, but that doesn't mean it might not happen again. Again, I will remind you to consider the professional intervention. It is a small investment to make when so much is at stake.

Chapter 10

The Fur is Flying
What Should You Do If Your Efforts to Integrate Fail?

Perhaps you've added a new dog to your crew and everything went okay at first. Maybe the honeymoon even lasted longer than just at first. But now fights seem to be the order of the day and nothing you are doing is making things better. Well, the first thing you should do in this case is to get professional behavior assistance. Books just don't do this situation justice. If you have two dogs who are trying to do bodily harm to one another, this is a dangerous situation for the entire household and cannot be ignored. Remember what I said about your dogs trusting you to keep them safe? That is really important here, particularly with the resident dogs who were there first. When the new kid on the block is causing problems, you do not want trust to be destroyed.

Of course, placing blame is not productive for anyone so don't bother doing that for long if at all. Just get help. And until you get help, keep the battling dogs apart, via a baby gate system, secure doors, etc. If you have children, this is even more important. Be proactive and take NO chances. Only a dog behavior specialist who is right there observing the

Fighting among your crew necessitates an immediate call to a professional. Keep those involved separated until you get assistance. If the fights are between dogs who got along just fine for a long time and suddenly started fighting, a medical workup should be a priority for all dogs involved. Document the circumstances surrounding each incident for the behavior professional.

situation can tell you what is going on and what might be the best course of action. Be sure to choose someone skilled at this type of work. See the resources section for websites to help you choose a local trainer.

If you have dogs who were getting along just fine and then suddenly, that is no longer the case, then all dogs involved should get full medical work ups. Write up a list of any changes in each dog's behavior and take it with you to your vet. Write up another list of any changes in the routine, no matter how small. You never know what triggers such changes and anything could be important. This list of information about the changes in routines should include not just the dog's routine but any changes in the human's routine as that also affects the dogs in the home. Show this list to the trainer that you choose, along with the behavior list.

What happens after you have worked with the professional and things are not improving? Maybe you got some forward movement but things are still not going very smoothly. Now is the time to make a decision. Plenty of people live in households with two dogs who don't get along or cannot even be in the same room for that matter. They live lives filled with baby gates and sturdy doors and crates and rotating dogs. They have much more to do than even the average multiple dogs household and they are okay with this. They live with the potential for tragedy daily. Is this a choice you are willing to make?

If surrendering a dog to another home is not something you can consider, then you need to spend some time thinking about whether you can live the life of rotating dogs. Again, this is especially important not only if you have children in your home but if you have a partner or others living in the home who may not be as much of a dog person as you are. They may not be comfortable with the rules and structure that will be needed to live such a life. And certainly children can throw a wrench into any such plan. They simply cannot be expected to understand the gravity of the situation and they are the ones who can be harmed the most, should things go terribly awry. Anyone who is not savvy about this situation can increase the likelihood of a mistake.

It is also important to note that this much tension takes a toll on all of the canine members of the household as well. It is very stressful to live on eggshells, always being aware that something very

If the medical workup is clear and the behavior professional gives you little hope for success, you have decisions to make. If you have the setup for it, you can live with feuding dogs but it takes an emotional toll on both humans and canines in the home alike. Think long and hard about whether you are willing to deal with this. Choosing what is best for all involved, especially the dogs, is the direction that you want to lean towards. Safety should be foremost.

bad can happen if someone makes a mistake. Living in a constant state of stress means always having elevated cortisol levels. This adds anxiety to any dog and/or human who may already be on the anxious side. It affects t he quality of life of everyone involved. Sadly, dogs cannot tell us when they feel this way so it's important for you to notice what their body language says to you. Remember, they trust you to be the ultimate benevolent leader. That means you are responsible for their well-being in all areas. Trust your instincts. Your decision must be based not only on what is best for the humans but also what is best for the dogs in the home.

So now you have entertained a thought to re-home a dog—something that you swore you would never do. You feel guilt-stricken and distraught but see no other viable option. It's important to understand that re-homing a dog is not a bad thing. It is not a failure. The bad thing would be not recognizing when this is the best option for all involved. Dogs are very adaptive, especially, if the dog that has prompted the issues is the newest. Who should you re-home? I strongly believe that it should always be the newest dog. The resident dog or dogs who have been there all along did not ask for the new crew member and do not deserve to lose their home because the new crew member has an issue with them or vice versa.

Remember, your dogs cannot talk with words so it is important for you to listen to their comments made the way that they make them. There is nothing more frustrating than being misunderstood. If the new dog is the one instigating the behavior, then re-homing the one who was there first is rewarding the inappropriate behavior. That shouldn't be your aim. Your aim is to restore harmony. Any discussion on re-homing should include your trainer, who can advise you of your options. Depending on how long you have had the new dog and where you got him from, you may be obligated to return him to a rescue group or shelter. If you adopted this dog from a shelter, many shelters are happy for responsible assistance in placement if perhaps you have an appropriate family member or friend who might be interested. That is always a great option and you can sometimes still see your former dog.

And if that does not turn out to be the case, you still should remember something. Just because you have made the decision to re-home a dog, does not mean that you have reneged on the commitment that you made to this dog when you took him in. You are still providing an appropriate and loving home for him. It just isn't going to be your home, because that is no longer what is best for him. And what is best all around is what is most important. Keep that thought first and foremost in your mind and avoid the guilt trips. It will be less stressful for you as well as the dogs. Your anxiety is noticeable to the dogs. The better you feel about your decision, the better the whole situation will flow.

> Re-homing a dog is not a failure. The failure would be to not recognize when there is a need to act. Dogs are very adaptable creatures. Loving means being able to let go when need be. Finding a dog a new home that works better for him is an act of love. If the fights involve a new addition to your home, that is the dog who should be re-homed. Remember, your crew trusts you. Reward that trust with safety and commitment.

Chapter 11

Tragedy in the Midst
Losing a Crew Member

One of the hardest things that any animal guardian ever faces is the passing of a beloved pet. It will also be hard on a multiple dog household because you are all a family, animals and humans alike. Whether the animal that passed away was a dog or even a cat, if will be often be equally difficult on the crew as a whole, especially if your dogs are as close with the felines in their lives as with the canines.

For ease of explanation, I will use the example of a dog passing for the rest of this section. The same advice would apply to other domestic animals as well, within the realm of practicality. Whether the passing was expected because of age or illness, or unexpected because of accident or sudden illness, it's a heart wrenching time.

When you have multiple dogs, this can be both a blessing and a curse. It is a blessing because you must remain among the world of the living in order to care for those who need you, and a curse because you must now also deal with your own grief and the grief of those who remain behind. This can be very frustrating since you can never fully know what your dogs understand as you try to explain.

Generally speaking, I am a big believer in talking to your dogs with a sort of regular conversation for certain scenarios. It is important to keep them apprised of what you think they might need to know or even just to point things out to them that you just feel like sharing with them. That concept applies here as well. I advise my clients to simply sit down with the remaining crew and tell them in words as kindly as you can what has happened. If the dog who passed away was sick and they were around for this, or if it was an accident or something that they witnessed, they very likely already know what happened to him, but that doesn't make them miss him any less.

If the rest of the crew has no first hand knowledge of what happened, things will be a bit harder for you. If it's possible, it is a good idea, for the well being of the remaining crew, for them to be able to see the body of the dog that passed away. This tells them all they need to know so that the grieving process can begin. If seeing the body is not possible, you can show them the dog's collar as well as the ashes when you pick them up.

If you opt to bury your dog yourself, here is your opportunity to have the rest of your crew share in the ceremony. Whether you choose to bury the whole body or just the ashes, I recommend that you have a ceremony. Have the deceased dog's belongings present. Show them to the rest of the crew, and do whatever kind of ceremony that makes you feel comfortable to honor that dog who passed. Let the others sniff the ash container and make a show of combining that with the honored dog's favorite collar and toys, etc. This can help to make the connection to the ashes for them.

You can expect a variety of reactions from your dogs, ranging from blasé to devastation. While you should be sure to not inadvertently reward feeling bad, you want to permit grieving. Grieving is normal. Be comforting with hugs and kisses and loving. Be understanding. But at the same time, encourage living as well. This will not only help the dog who is hurting, it will help you

Honor your dog's memory; don't lose yourself or your remaining crew members in grief. Do the things you did before your loss as much

Simply telling your crew why one of them is missing can be beneficial to the grieving process, especially if they have no direct knowledge of what transpired. Sharing a ceremony with the remaining crew will help them to transition to life without their friend. This is especially helpful if you are burying your dog on your property. Keep your crew's routine as best as you can in order to help your crew feel stability in shaky times. Being strong for your crew will also help you to come farther along than if you had to face this alone.

as possible. Be as normal as possible with your dogs. That will be the key to helping them feel back in the saddle. Dogs love routine. Routines help them feel safe. So stick to routines as much as possible in order to help them feel safe. It will go a long way towards helping you to feel safe again, too.

Times will be hard for a bit. It's up to you to lead your crew back to the light. Sometimes, the pain will be crushing, but the remaining crew will look to you for their cues. So do your best and be their light at the end of the tunnel. Make sure that you give them the love and affection and reassurance that they need now. It will be hard. You will be in the pain of loss yourself but you have the ability to verbalize that loss and they don't. You know all the details of why there is a loss and maybe they don't. So be their rock. Being their rock will give you stability as well.

Is it okay if you break down in front of them? Yes, of course. This happens to all of us. It very likely has happened long before your crew got split up by loss. Break down, hug them all close to you, and let them lick your face and get up and get on with your life as your lost canine love would want you to.

As far as different reactions go, do not for a minute think that if one of your dogs is blasé about the absence of the lost crew member that it means he doesn't care. If they were not enemies while the lost one was alive, regardless of what the blasé dog shows, he feels the loss. Just like humans, animals have different personalities and different ways of expressing their feelings. This will be the one you need to be most aware of in some cases, so you don't miss subtle symptoms of grief that the dog can't handle much longer. At the opposite end of the spectrum will be the one who is obviously mourning and roaming around the house searching and sniffing places the lost one frequented most often. They may look searchingly at you for answers. Be mindful of this behavior so the anxiety does not grow.

As mentioned earlier, routine will be so helpful towards getting things back on an even keel. Grief is important to express and process, so it's perfectly natural. Just know that it can sometimes get out of hand and as the leader of this crew, it's up to you keep your eyes open so that doesn't happen.

While in most cases, the remaining crew will be lost for a while, if the one who passed was a challenging crew member, you may see less anxiety in some of your dogs now. Things may be calmer all around. This can also be the case when your dog passes away because of either an illness or of the complications of age. This type of situation places great stress on a household and it can be a relief when the sick or troublesome dog passes, even though they were dearly loved. Please don't let this make you feel guilty. It happens. Consider what you have learned from the dog who is gone and be grateful for the opportunity you have had to learn more about how that dog's personality affected the remaining crew. You will have learned something valuable for that time when you are ready to add another member to your crew. Consider your loss part of life's growing pains.

While I am not the type of trainer who subscribes to the whole pack theory scenario, there is no getting around the fact that there are leaders and there are followers, both in the human and the canine world. While the whole thing that many call dominance is fluid in a family, when a leader is the one who passed away, it does upset the balance of the crew.

You are the ultimate leader but the most confident dogs in your crew will also be leaders of sorts. The loss of a leader can create more of a void with followers. They have less to lean on and may be the ones I described who are wandering around looking the most lost. It is important now to make sure that you don't get any jostling now from dogs whom I like to call second lieutenants. These are the dogs with confidence issues who think they might have leadership abilities but in actuality, they lack the confidence to handle the position. This is an important time to remind everyone that you are the

You may see a variety of reactions among your crew. This is normal. Just as with people, there will be ranges from obviously seeking the departed to completely normal. In some cases, you may see relief such as in the case of a dog who was a challenge to live with or one who was ill for a long time. Dispense with the guilt if this is the case. This is a normal reaction. If you have lost a leader type dog, your crew may be out of sorts. Make sure that they look to you for direction. Prevent inappropriate jostling for the empty position.

benevolent leader. Be calm, be confident and be there for them. Use posture and body movements to direct things if need be and just love them all.

Another loss to consider is the loss of a human crew member be it from death or a break up of sorts. Either way, this also creates a void. The person is gone from the life of your dogs or perhaps their time together has been greatly reduced. The same grieving process applies. If a death has occurred, this is often easier to show the dog than with the death of a canine housemate. Make friends with your funeral director so that you can have a few precious moments to show your beloved dogs what happened.

I realize that what I am asking will be hard while you are in the middle of your own heartache. It will save you some searching, however, if you can gather the strength to be aware in your time of grief. If the person is gone because of a break up, be aware that there can be some acting out behavior when you start dating again. The same can apply with a death, but usually more time has passed before the dating begins. Again, the more you stick with the rest of your routine, the more smoothly the transition will be. And making sure that the attention that you give your crew is plentiful will help them to cope.

> If you have lost a human crew member, it can often be easier to allow your crew to see departed if he did not pass at home. If the loss is due to a break up, expect potential acting out when you begin dating again. Again sticking with routines can make a huge difference. You will know when you are ready to add another canine crew member. Listen to your gut.

When is it appropriate to add a new canine crew member when you have lost one? That will vary according to what is right for you. There is no universal answer to that question. You will know when you are ready. Some people cannot even begin to think of getting another dog while they are in heavy mourning. Others cannot have a void in their lives and need to fill it asap. Please try very hard to think of your other crew members' needs when you make this decision. The ramifications are important and your choices should be made with clarity.

As for what to look for in a new canine housemate, refer to the section on this subject. However, a point to keep in mind is leadership. If you lost a leader dog, choose another leader dog. Not a pushy shovey "it's all about me" dog, but a dog that has natural confidence but also kindness and will have the respect of the other dogs. If you already have follower dogs, adding another follower will likely give you more anxiety. Can you mold them? Sure, but you had better be a strong and confident benevolent leader.

Chapter 12

And Puppy Makes Three
Adding a New Dog to Your Home

You've decided to add a new dog to your household. How do you choose what kind of personalities to mix up? Well, consider the temperaments of your resident dogs first. If your dogs are not terribly friendly to strange dogs, then adding another dog to the mix is not a good idea at this time. You should tend to your dogs' unfriendliness first. There are many effective trainers and great training books to help you with that. But if your dogs ARE social, then you can start by going to a shelter and seeing what kind of dog appeals to you. Then bring your own dogs in for a meet-and-greet. Most shelters and especially most rescue groups have personnel or volunteers who are trained in matching people and animals together and they can observe and offer suggestions.

If you have found a potential new crew member via a private party, make sure

> If your crew is wary of new canine playmates, hire a professional to assist you in choosing a new crew member. Be sure to have the initial meeting on neutral ground. Be familiar with the breed traits of your current crew, particularly the more confident members. Know whether you have a breed with potential same sex aggression issues to prevent a future problem. Sometimes more important than breed traits, is the confidence levels of your crew. Be sure to not place a super confident dog in a household of skittish dogs and vice versa.

that you have someone with you, preferably a professional, who is familiar with canine body language, when you have the meeting. It's important to do this correctly, especially when there are several personalities to take into account. Meetings held on neutral ground are best. If your dogs are choosy about their playmates, it would be well worth it to hire a professional to accompany you on a meet-and-greet. I offer this service for my clients and it can save you heartache later.

You can try and perfectly match your current dogs' personalities to the newcomers, but that is not a necessity. You can have several dogs with differing personalities and energy levels living happily together. If you only have one dog, in most cases I suggest adding a dog of the opposite sex, as discussed in a previous chapter. In a multiple dog household, if you already have one of each, then obviously you will have one more of one sex shortly.

However, consider which breeds you already have. Some breeds have a propensity to posture with the other members of their sex, either solely amongst that breed or in other males of other breeds as well. Know your breeds, even if you have mixes. It will make a difference in some cases. Plenty of households who have all males or all females have no issues. Just be aware that sometimes sex can make a difference. I personally think it's easier to have multiple females rather than multiple males, but there will be just as many people who say the opposite.

Another important thing to keep in mind when matching new dogs to your household is the confidence level of your dogs. If you currently have skittish dogs and want to add a very confident dog to your household, this could easily cause a problem. If you are not interested in monitoring their every interaction very closely, you might want to choose a less confident dog.

It is very easy for shy dogs to be overwhelmed with a pushy dog and it's not fair to the shy dogs. They were there first and although the rank structure among the canines should not be a big issue, the dogs who are already in the home should come first when you are deciding on new additions to your crew. Your dogs need to be reassured that nothing about your love and affection for them changes with a newcomer. If you currently have very confident dogs, adding a more subdued dog is often the best choice. There are many subtleties to consider but thoroughly believing that you can handle the whole multiple dog thing well will be your best recipe for success.

What if you find a stray dog that you want to keep (after contacting all the right people to determine that he is indeed lacking a home of his own, of course!)? Well, that can be your best dream come true or your worst nightmare. Not every successful mix will be successful from day one, so a good or bad first day may not be your best indicator of whether it will work in the long run. You may have to do some integration work, but you can usually get an accurate sense of how it will go within a day or two.

In the beginning, if either the newcomer or one of your current dogs are reacting so strongly that you fear for someone's safety, that is a bad sign. Get professional help if you are determined to try to see this through. But keep in mind that it is not a failure if you cannot make a new addition work.

> If you have chosen to try and keep a dog you have found, be sure to contact all proper authorities to report finding the dog first. If you think things might blend smoothly between your crew and your foundling with a little assistance, then either hire a professional or get a dog savvy friend to help you integrate them.

Choosing a new dog to join your home is a momentous decision. You are choosing family members here. Dogs are not born into the family like your human family and you have an opportunity to create harmony in the home among everyone. Experiencing stress on a daily basis is not good for anyone, human or canine. If you foresee stress and chaos as a result of the foundling, even through no fault of his own, it is a responsible act to find a better forever home for him. If you prefer not to subject the dog to a shelter, find a rescue group to assist you with placing him in a more appropriate home. Try conducting an internet search using Petfinder to find assistance in your area. If you are going to keep the dog in your home while you search for a new home for him, you must ensure everyone's safety so make the proper accommodations.

What if your foundling and your current dogs seem like they might get along just fine with a little help? Success often lies with how you integrate them. If the dog is already in your house, then telling you to have your own dogs meet the newcomer on neutral grounds is a moot point. But if you have simply separated your dogs and the newcomer with baby gates and doors, and the outcome has been okay but not warm and fuzzy yet, you have hope.

First, get some dog-savvy human assistance if you live alone. Gather the family and some leashes and high value treats if you don't. Be creative! Think about what your dogs like best. Diet is covered more thoroughly in a previous chapter but let me mention again now that any highly processed treat that contains sugar and preservatives is not a good choice to use in this situation. Treats like this have the potential to cause hyperactivity and that is not what you need here. You need zen!

If thus far the integrated mix ups have gone reasonably well, get all the responsible adults together and have leashes for every dog. Choose a room where you typically relax, such as a living room/ family room. It is best that this room is large enough that the dogs, while on leash, cannot reach each other in a state of relaxation, perhaps even stretched out. Match each dog with a leash and a human handler. Each person will have high value treats. If anyone, human or canine, has any anxiety at all over this process, I suggest that you take some or all of the following measures to ensure that the anxiety is reduced.

Reduce anxiety in the canines by adding some of the natural calming remedies that were discussed in a previous section. Start with D.A.P. Comfort Zone® or Chill Out Spray. Spray D.A.P.® liberally on the soft surfaces in the room, or spray Chill Out liberally around the room before the dogs enter the room (or even once they've joined you, taking care to not spray them directly into the faces, of

> Creating good associations between your crew and your foundling requires setting the stage. Gather enough hands for all the leashes, have clickers and high value treats handy. Use all the calming remedies recommended that you can and go to work. This may take more than one integration session or it may not. Go at the dog's speed, not yours. Never make assumptions regarding their readiness to be all together without supervision. Better safe than sorry. This part can take months and it can sometimes be never (unsupervised, that is).

course! Bach's Rescue Remedy® will really be handy, especially if you don't use this on a regular basis. Dose each dog approximately fifteen minutes prior to the meeting. For most uses, two to four drops or sprays directly into the mouth should do the trick. The humans who are anxious can also use it.

When the scene is properly set, proceed according to the personalities of the dogs involved. The most confident or pushy dog should be paired with the most confident human present. If you know how to use a clicker, that is a great addition to this training scenario. Every single time the dogs that might be wary of the newcomer look at him, you click and treat. Or you can verbally mark and treat. I prefer the clicker for this type of situation, if the dogs are familiar with it, as it is more unbiased than a voice. Occasionally, a dog can be afraid of the clicker's sound, so use whatever marker works best for you if that is the case.

Do this with the newcomer at the same time. Everyone should find this a positive and pleasing experience. You want them all to associate being around each other with yummy high value treats. This needs to be done numerous times on a daily basis until you feel comfortable that there will be no issues. It should be done in any room where you regularly spend time, including the bedroom if your dogs sleep with you.

Ruby (min pin), Oskar, Takoda & Jasmine relaxed together. Jasmine (snoozing on the chair) is the newest addition.

It is important that you do not make assumptions too soon about how well everyone gets along. Supervision is really important! Someone must be around to ensure that any inappropriate behavior is interrupted before it becomes an issue. Trust your gut feelings; they rarely lie to you. When everyone is comfortable around one another in a relaxation mode, you will feel it. Everything else will flow from there.

Chapter 13

Proofing the Pups
The Training Basics Explained

This section is not intended to replace professional training assistance, particularly if you have serious behavior issues among your crew that need to be addressed in person. The information contained here can help you understand the basics of positive reinforcement training, including some step-by-step instructions. I will not go into great detail explaining why this type of training works better than traditional training, nor will I provide any detailed scientific data. My aim is simply to provide some basic assistance to help you smoothly maintain a multiple dog household. For any serious issues, please contact a professional. Please see the resources section of this book to locate additional information on various subjects that can assist you.

The more dogs you have, the more it will help you to know all that you can in relation to your dogs. Don't hesitate to read all that interests you and perhaps some materials that don't. Every bit of knowledge will assist you in better handling a multiple dog household. The same goes for professional training. There is no such thing as too much training, especially when you have multiple dogs. Seek classes in your geographic area and don't forget about in-home training for any behavior issues that are not addressed in a class setting.

Starting with the leadership portion below, these are the handouts that I give to my training clients. Most of them I wrote in entirety; others were originally or partially written by fellow trainers that I work with including Lori Caruso, Lilian Akin and Barb Grosch, but I revised them to suit my own beliefs and style. I have given them credit where appropriate.

This first section expands upon some of what I have already mentioned, benevolent leadership. It outlines why it is important and as well as the methods for establishing yourself as the benevolent leader for your dogs. Your goal is to encourage your dogs to look to you for direction, particularly when they are anxious or distracted. Call it whatever you want to as long as you implement it similarity to what I have described.

Benevolent Leadership

One of the dictionary definitions of benevolence is as follows:

THE DISPOSITION TO DO GOOD; GOOD WILL; CHARITABLENESS; LOVE OF MANKIND, ACCOMPANIED WITH A DESIRE TO PROMOTE THEIR HAPPINESS. [1]

This is the basis of good leadership. Leadership isn't about dominance or showing that you are the top dog. It is about running things with the happiness of everyone as a whole in mind. It's about gentle guidance. It's about being able to think about the big picture. To do that, rules for behavior are very important. Politeness and manners ensure that everyone gets along well.

Politeness and manners can be emphasized throughout your daily life with your dog. Teaching impulse control is something every dog needs to learn. The key to successful benevolent leadership is instilling manners in your dog, so he has a behavior to fall back on. Once you convey to your dog that you are the provider of all; that you take care of all needs, that you solve all problems, etc., your dog feels confident that he only need look to you for direction. You will be building respect for your leadership but you will also be respectful of the partnership that you and your dog are building together. Being a benevolent leader that your dog can trust is the key to building the best relationship with your dog that you possibly can. Having a successful relationship with your dog is the ultimate basis for having a well trained dog.

---

1   Webster's 1913 Dictionary (www.webster-dictionary.org). Derived from the Webster's Revised Unabridged Dictionary Version published 1913 by the C. & G. Merriam Co. Springfield, Mass. Under the direction of Noah Porter, D.D., LL.D.

Key points to remember:

•Teach your dog to ask for everything he wants until it becomes second nature; i.e.: sit to be served meals; sit to be let out; wait for a cue to go out of a door or other opening: sit for petting; be polite about couch and bed access. You can ask for more than a sit. For high energy dogs, teaching a default down results in more politeness.

•Raised surfaces such as human beds and couches are resources that need to be earned. They should be off-limits to any dog that you are having compliance problems with. However, there is no reason to limit your dog's access to beds and couches if you are not having such a problem. Enjoy his company there if you desire!

•Be in charge of play. If the excitement level is getting too high, stop the play and issue a "Settle" period, even if you have to leash your dog to you and sit quietly to obtain this. Reward for calm behavior. If calm comes easy, the reward can be a return to play.

•Reward your dog every time he looks to you for direction. In the same vein, reward your dog every time he offers polite behavior without being asked. Rewards don't mean just food. They should include praise, affection, play and life rewards, more so than food during the course of an average day. But food should definitely play a large part in rewards, especially for specific training. Good leaders lead without bribery, but they always reward lavishly! Make it the most wonderful thing in the world to please you and you will set the stage for success.

You and your dog are in this together. You are not adversaries. Your job is to look out for your dog and to teach him that you will handle every situation successfully, so he need never worry. Of course, training your dog involves teaching him to problem-solve and think on his own to determine what behavior YOU want, but you have the final say.

That is what true leadership and guidance is all about. Good leaders guide without dictating or smothering. Good leaders don't punish mistakes, they reward successes. Good leaders make following fun. Good leaders inspire their followers. It is up to you to be the most interesting game in town!

What Does Positive Training Mean?

In this section, my colleague Lori Caruso provided the inspiration for the positive training intro paragraph. She also initially wrote the luring section which was later edited and added to by me to show my preferences.

While positive reinforcement training is based on solid scientific studies, it is also based on real life. Consider this real-life scenario. You go to work, for the most part, because you get paid to do so. The paycheck is the primary incentive. And for most people, it is a strong one! But your boss doesn't have to waive money in front of your face all day to get you to do your job, right? It's the same with positive training. It's not all about the food. Of course, food is used and in the beginning, it's used quite a bit. But the object is to reward, not to bribe. It's a paycheck as well as bonuses for extra special performances.

What else can happen at the workplace that becomes an incentive? Well, being told that you did a great job! What does that do? It creates a feeling of happiness and confidence, and a desire to recreate that feeling as much as possible. That is what you are doing for your dog when you acknowledge his appropriate behavior. Combining food with a verbal marker and/or a clicker helps your dog to connect his good behavior with earning their paycheck.

Rewards help a dog learn that his behavior has consequences and it gives him a feeling of control over the outcome. You are creating a happier and more confident dog, a dog that is aware of what choices he can make to get that warm and fuzzy feeling. You are also cementing a strong relationship with your dog. How does that work? Well, when you consistently let your dog know what you expect of him, he is better able to trust that he is safe and secure. He can gather all the information that you can offer to create a routine. Dogs love routines. Routines offer safety and security.

When dogs are confused, they can feel anxious. Be very clear about what makes you happy as far as your dog's behavior goes. You will create a secure and confident dog who knows how to do what you want. When your dog knows he can count on you to give good instructions, he will always look to you for more information.

You will be making life fun for your dog. And you will be giving your dog a behavior routine that will help him feel secure when his life routine is disrupted because of unforeseen circumstances. This is a win/win situation all around.

Let's look at the other side of this coin. When you have a bad experience, you generally try very hard to avoid having that happen again. This is our survival instinct at its finest. The same goes for dogs. Dogs do not deliberately choose to upset us. They simply do not know what behavior we want. It's up to us to teach them what we want, and that includes teaching them the words that we use to convey the behavior we seek. Most dogs do not come to us, for the most part, knowing what words mean. We add meaning to the words. It's up to us to connect the words with the behaviors we want. We must add meaning in such a way that we make the words valuable information rather than simply babbling at our dogs. Dogs will quickly learn to tune us out, or even worse, they will become anxious when they upset us, because we have chosen to correct rather than instruct.

Most people want their relationship with their dog to improve. Positive training will not only help that to happen, it will also prevent your dog from becoming afraid of you because he did not understand what you tried to convey to him. Punishment works, but with a price. And part of that price is often damage to the trust in the relationship. Positive training builds trust and deepens your relationship, and there is nothing but good that can come from that combo! It makes training not only fun for your dog, but fun for you as well!

So let's get on with how we implement this wonderful thing known as positive reinforcement training!

When you are learning to teach a dog via positive reinforcement training, there are two important terms that you must learn: capturing and luring.

Capturing

Capturing is the most important way to train your dog with positive reinforcement methods. Capturing basically means that you will catch your dog behaving well. You will mark his good behavior and reward it. You can do this at any time. You just need your mouth or a clicker, or you can use both. To use your voice most effectively to teach your dog what you like, you will need to use a marker word so we will address that first. A marker word is a word spoken to mark or capture the exact instant your dog does the desired behavior. If you want to use a clicker to mark good stuff, that's great; just use the clicker where you read that the marker word should be used. But I believe that it is also important to learn how to use a marker word as well. I use both depending on the dog and what I want him to learn. Once you have taught a behavior using the clicker, you can switch to a marker word for maintenance.

The clicker is the best tool for teaching many new behaviors and for proofing a behavior in high distraction circumstances when the dog already knows a behavior. Proofing simply means that you make the behavior solid. The difference between a clicker and a marker word is that the clicker never lies (or shouldn't!). If you click, you treat, period. That is what makes it so powerful. That is also why I typically reserve it for new and/or harder to teach behaviors. If you verbally mark, you always treat when you are FIRST teaching a behavior, but you will learn to treat at random times once you have taught a behavior. And you can progress from a marker word such as "yes!" to more general verbal praise such as "good boy!" when your dog has developed solid behavior repetition.

When choosing a marker word, pick a word that is one syllable and that you can remember easily. It need not make sense to anyone but you and your dog. Some commonly used words are "Yes!", "Good!", "Nice!" or "Yay!" You can even make up a word if you choose. Choosing a word that you can single out to use in this circumstance rather than one you use a lot throughout the day is a good idea. The more distinctive the word is, and the more expressively you say it (in a very happy excited tone, for example), the more readily your dog will pay attention. The marker word itself is not as important to your dog as what it signifies. To your dog, it will mean good things happen when they hear it. You seem happy when you say that word and a happy dog mom or dad means a happy dog.

What is important about using your marker word is the timing. Whatever behavior you mark is the behavior that you will get MORE of. So it is important to work on your timing. You can practice this in several everyday situations, but one of the best times is while you are sitting at a traffic light waiting for a green light. Go ahead and shout out your marker word at the exact moment that the light changes to green. You won't see those people in the car next to you again and you will perfect your timing, making it much easier to train your dog well.

You are going to pair your marker word with a reward. In most cases, especially when training a new behavior, the reward will mean a high value treat. You will learn to capture all of your dog's desirable behavior and mark it with your word, quickly following that with a treat. Your dog will start looking for opportunities to earn hearing that word. For example, when you're teaching your dog to sit, as soon as his behind touches the ground you say your marker word happily to let your dog know that was the behavior you wanted, and then give him a treat.

Because humans and dogs do not speak the same language, we need to communicate with them in ways they will understand that do not create trauma. Using a marker word makes training fun and gives your dog a goal. Having a marker word makes it easier for your dog to understand exactly what behavior he is being rewarded for.

I cannot stress how important timing is for successfully capturing behavior. When you only mark the behavior with a treat, then the time delay between when the dog performs the behavior and when you give the dog the treat can create confusion. In that short span of time, the dog may have done several other things like wag his tail, look at something across the room or stand up again, so when you do give the treat, your dog may not be exactly sure which behavior earned him the treat. Having a marker word makes it crystal clear that the behavior he performed at the exact moment he heard the marker word is the desired behavior. The marker word helps connect the behavior and the word in your dog's mind much more easily.

Your dog learns that your marker word is a cue that he just did something that you liked. He will come to learn that this word is a good thing. He will try to elicit the word from you, because hearing that word will create a happy moment for him. Say that you are having a problem luring your dog into a sit. Place your dog on a leash and try luring him into a sit. If your dog is not getting it, wait until he sits of his own free will. He will very likely do this pretty quickly because he will be confused by what you want and not know what else to do. When he sits, say "yes!" in the happiest party voice you can muster, and then present him with a treat. After a few repetitions of this, you will see a light bulb go off. Your dog will connect the word and the behavior.

An important note about the timing of the treat: using a "sit" as an example, if your dog has gotten up by the time your hand gets to him with the treat, simply wordlessly pull back the treat and wait until he sits again, then bring the treat closer again. Repeat as needed.

Again try luring him into this position, perhaps with a hand signal. If he sits, mark the behavior and reward him. The next time, say the word "sit" just BEFORE he sits and again, mark and reward. And the sit on cue is born! All because you "caught" him sitting and he discovered that it benefited you both. How easy is that?

The best thing about capturing and marking good behavior in your dog it is that it forces him to think about what he did to get such a great response. Capturing teaches your dog that there are consequences to his actions. HE can make good things happen. What a great thing for him to know!

In addition to simply capturing single behaviors, capturing has another purpose. Capturing behaviors allows you to use one behavior to teach another related behavior. You can create what is called a behavior chain by doing this. It's a simple process that your dog perceives as a game, and that makes it pleasant and fun. No stress involved! It's just you and your dog learning new things together.

For example, perhaps you have taught your dog to step on a mat in order to get a treat. Your goal is to teach him to lie down on the mat, so after he has learned to step on the mat consistently, you up the ante. Have two levels of rewards: good treats and better treats. For the stepping on the mat that he already knows, he gets the good treat. A behavior that is closer to what you ultimately want, such as a play bow, will gain him a better treat. Mark and reward that behavior and proceed until your dog reaches the goal behavior. When your dog grasps the ultimate goal, he should get a "jackpot".

A jackpot is a larger amount of treats than is typical for a marked behavior, such as ten treats instead of one. These are delivered in a rapid succession, not in a lump. Dogs like jackpots. They are memorable and that is what you want. So when you get that extra behavior, give your dog that jackpot and create a memorable moment. Once he is offering this new behavior reliably, you can name this new behavior. To successfully name the new behavior, you would strive to say the name just as he is about to perform the behavior. Be careful to not use the cue words you want to combine with behaviors, before your dog has learned the behaviors. Using the cue word before the dog is performing the behavior regularly will do what we call poison the cue. It will make the word meaningless so be aware of how you use words that you want your dog to attach meaning to. Less is definitely more in this instance! Repeating cues over and over again also falls into this category.

As mentioned earlier, you can use either a marker word or a clicker. It's up to you. I do not usually use a clicker to teach basic behaviors like a "sit" or other easy behaviors unless there is a twist, such as asking for a behavior when distractions are a problem, or if a dog is having a harder time understanding what I want. I do use a clicker when practicing pure shaping behavior that is being done just for fun. As noted earlier, if you want to use a clicker, the clicker clicks at the same time that the marker word would is spoken (only using one or the other!) but in many situations, the clicker is a clearer signal to the dog.

Once you have instilled some behaviors in your dog, I recommend a three-level rewarding system. For example, the lowest level means that every single action you ask your dog to do that he completes should be acknowledged. If it's a simple sit that he knows very well inside the house with no distractions, then the marker/reward should usually be a happy-sounding "good boy" (or "good girl").

For the second level, if it is something your dog is not consistently performing yet or if it's a simple sit that he does outside that he complies with most of the time, that would get a "yes!" or other marker word that you have chosen. Sometimes you combine this word with a treat and sometimes you don't. The instances where your dog performs the requested behavior fast would definitely elicit a treat! Once behaviors are learned, "yes" becomes like a slot machine, sometimes delivering a treat and sometimes not. This keeps your dog working in the hope that that will be the time he gets the treat. When it is a harder behavior for him to complete and he still does it, he should get a treat.

The highest level of marking a behavior is with a clicker. So any behavior that warrants a click, ALWAYS gets a treat. Remember, the clicker never lies. If you click, you treat, period. That is why the clicker is reserved for harder to teach behaviors or behaviors that happen when the situation is distracting. For example, if your dog sees a squirrel and he still looks at you when requested to, that warrants a click and a high value treat.. Does this make your brain spin? Don't worry! You will get it, just like your dog. It's fun to play the capture and reward game.

Lures and Rewards Explained

The second and sometimes more commonly used way to train your dog with positive training is called lure and reward. How do you use lure and reward training? Very simple! Find something your dog likes and use it to lure him into performing various behaviors and then reward him for compliance. Many things can be used as lures and rewards. Keep reading for that list. It is important, however to understand the difference between a lure and a bribe. If your dog is barking at something while facing away from you and you go to his face and show him a tasty treat to quiet him, that is a bribe. If you wait until he glances your way or move in such a way that he looks at you and then you show him a treat to entice him away from the direction that he is barking, then that is a lure. If he moves in the direction that you want and you give him the treat when he comes with you, that is a reward. Simple, right? Food lures get faded out pretty quickly once the learning begins so don't worry about over-feeding.

A lure is very useful when teaching new behaviors, overcoming confusion or fear on the dog's part, and as a means of increasing the interest in what you are trying to teach them. A lure can be a quick way to establish a relationship and gain cooperation with a dog. A lure is offered before a behavior is elicited and either directly assists in guiding/shaping the behavior or minimizing/eliminating the stumbling blocks of confusion or fear.

You can choose lures and rewards from a variety of things that your dogs love. Make a list. Food is one thing that most dogs love and it's easy to carry around. Toys, petting, and praise can also be positive reinforcers. But food is usually the most valuable reward you can give your dog. Verbal praise is definitely a necessity, but it usually is not motivating enough alone for most dogs when they are just learning a new behavior, especially when distractions rear their ugly head. Toys are great rewards as well, but using them as a reward can take more time because you have to stop and let your dog play. Using food is usually the most convenient for luring and rewarding, but your dog must be interested in the lure. If you think that your dog doesn't like treats, try a different one! All dogs like to eat. You just need to find the treat that is more exciting than the distraction.

What kinds of high value rewards should you use? As far as commercial soft treats, the more natural, the better. Avoid those unnaturally colored treats that are grocery store staples, especially if you have a very high-energy dog. They are full of sugar and preservatives and they are sure to make your hyper-active dog even more so. For more treat recommendations, see further in this chapter.

Most dogs have a favorite treat. Be creative to discover what it is. You can even make your own treats; recipes are included in this chapter for a few types of treats. Dry biscuits are great for rewarding your dog for just being who he is, but when you are training, you need small soft treats so you don't have to stop and wait for the crunching to be over. This is one instance where inhaling the food is better!

Another type of reward is something called a "life reward." A life reward involves allowing your dog to do what he wants as a reward for good behavior that you want. Life rewards can be as simple as having your dog sit before he walks through a door (the reward for sitting is getting to go through the door) or having a dog sit before he gets up on the couch (the reward for sitting is getting up on the couch), having your dog sit before throwing a Frisbee (the reward for sitting is getting to chase the Frisbee), or having your dog stop pulling before you continue walking (the reward for not pulling is continuing on the walk). By using a life reward you can strengthen a behavior that the dog might not want to do by allowing him to do something he really wants to do. I require one of my dogs to look at me when he wants to stop and sniff anything in depth.

Lures can be the same food items that you use to reward, but lures are best utilized just to get the dog started. The quick rule of thumb is to lure three times to get the dog interested in training. It's hard for a dog to concentrate on what we want him to do if there is a chunk of food hanging over him! All he can think about is that chunk of food in his face. It's far more effective to use the food as a reward rather than overuse it as a lure.

Likewise, avoid letting your dog become accustomed to seeing your bait bag or an open container of food on the table ready to reward him. Rewards should be anticipated but not always expected once a behavior is learned. You will learn to be random, like a slot machine, so that your dog thinks he might win, so he plays along. The payment always comes but the substance can vary. In the beginning, the food rewards are constant.

Now that you know what lures and rewards are, how do you use them appropriately?

Treats & rewards can be used to lure a dog into a position. Once your dog performs the behavior, reward him. Your goal is to get your dog to respond properly without having to reward him with food every time. But there should always be a verbal acknowledgment.

The key to using rewards effectively is to vary them; don't always give the same treat or use the same food, toy or game. Be more interesting than anything else around you!

It is important to reward with a "jackpot" as appropriate. Remember, an extra large number of treats makes an extra big impression on the dog and greatly increases the likelihood of a repeat performance. For an example of when a jackpot is appropriate; if your dog immediately responds to you in a distracting situation, a jackpot is a necessity! Get your dog's attention with that and he will respond just as quickly the next time.

The idea is to quickly (three time rule!) phase out the use of treats as a lure, and to go to a random use of treats as rewards. You never completely stop giving treats. Remember, you want your dog to think of you as a slot machine. He never can tell when he will get a reward, so he does what you ask because he might get one. After all, the treats are part of his paycheck and paychecks don't stop when you know your job well, do they?

So how do you prevent creating a dog who will only listen when you have a treat in your hand? One way is to rely much more heavily on capturing than on luring. But some dogs or situations simply require a lure. So you can prevent needing a lure by practicing patience and simply waiting for the behavior once you have gotten it a couple of times with a lure. This makes the treat a reward rather than a lure. Stop using the treats as a lure as soon as possible, but continue using the treats as a reward.

When you can reliably get your dog to change positions (sit, stand, down, etc.) with a lure in your hand, it is time to stop using the lure. Continue moving your hand as though it still holds the lure, as a hand signal for the dog. Keep the treat hidden in your other hand, or a pocket until the dog completes the behavior. Then mark the behavior and give the treat to your dog. Have a party and tell him how wonderful he is!

At this point, you can also start asking more of your dog for a reward. This is called raising the criteria. You need not necessarily do both of these at the same time. Set your dog up for success. Instead of giving a treat every time, give one every other time, then every third time, etc. It's hard to be totally random, but try not create a pattern the dog might inadvertently learn.

Work your way up to increasing the criteria for a treat, such as only giving your dog treats for the best/fastest responses. If your dog does a down very quickly, give a treat. But if he responds to the cue slowly, he gets no food reward: just a verbal acknowledgment. This sends a clear message to your dog: the quickest, most accurate performance gets the best rewards. Most dogs pick up on this concept quickly.

Quick Reference Guide to Proper Reward Usage

The following is a summary of the key points to keep in mind when doling out rewards. It's easy to go overboard and it's equally easy to be too stingy. Striking the proper balance in using rewards will get you the best outcome. I do want to stress that you should ALWAYS verbally reward every single behavior you ask for. The rewards I am referring to below are food and other higher value rewards.

- Raise your criteria. Require more behaviors before you dole out a reward. Example: once your dog knows a solid sit, add a down to the behavior before doling out a reward.
- Be unpredictable; keep your dog guessing when he will be getting a treat after an already learned behavior is performed.

Sometimes he does and sometimes he doesn't. Reward especially fast compliance more than so-so compliance. Reward compliance that is harder for the dog, such as when there is a distraction nearby. You get the idea!

- Rewarding behavior as randomly as humanly possible makes the behavior stronger because your dog never knows when the reward is coming. The uncertainty of not being rewarded with food every single time he offers a behavior will often lead to faster and more enthusiastic responses to elicit the food reward.
- Vary the treats you offer. Have a wide variety commonly available.
- Offer a reward other than a treat on a regular but randomly chosen basis. Know what your dog considers a reward. Make a list and choose from it on a frequent basis.
- Vary which hand you provide a reward from. Suppress your desire to use your dominant hand all the time.
- Vary which place on your person that you produce a reward from. Learn to like clothing with ample pockets.
- Vary where you produce your rewards from. Periodically ask your dog to perform a behavior, mark it and then go get the food reward from another room or from a hidden drawer or cupboard.
- It is important to make sure that rewards are not always visible once the behavior is learned. Your dog can easily learn that offering a behavior when no food reward is visible can mean there will be no reward. Be sure to prove differently.

Being unpredictable with the when, what and where of rewards will create an interested dog who is willing to offer you desirable behaviors in order to entice you to produce those rewards.

ATTENTION CUE

Now we come to the step-by-step cues that I provide to my clients. The first of these is an "attention to the handler" cue.

OBJECT: To teach your dog how to drop everything and look directly at you when you say your Attention Cue.

INSTRUCTION:

- Choose your Attention Cue word and Marker Word (or use a clicker).
- Most common Attention Cue choices are "watch" or "look" but be aware of whether you use either of these or another possible choice in another context throughout the day. Also, avoid choosing a word that sounds like another cue you use (example: touch and watch) Strive to avoid confusion!
- Get your high value treats of choice clutched in each hand.
- Position your dog directly in front of you, facing you. If your dog is too active to try this off leash, you can stand on your leash so you have both hands free.
- Show your dog the treats in both of your hands.
- Extend both arms parallel to the floor, like you are pretending to have wings.
- Stand up straight. Do not lean over your dog.
- Say your dog's name in a happy and inviting tone of voice.
- The moment that your dog looks into your eyes, say your Marker Word immediately in a very happy tone and treat immediately after.
- If your dog does not respond immediately when you say his name, make interesting noises to get his attention such as a kissing noise, a bird-like noise or any noise that does the trick.
- Do not use your attention cue word of choice until your dog is responding regularly to your attempts at getting his attention. Once he's done it several times in a row reliably, then you can add the cue. Say the cue word after his name, but before he looks your way. If he does not respond right away, do not repeat the cue. Go to your repertoire of funny noises and mark when he does look your way.

TIPS:

- Practice this over and over and over with your dog. The more you practice this cue and make it like a game, the more automatic your dog's Attention Cue behavior will become. I recommend a couple of minutes daily.
- Once your dog is consistently looking in your eyes, say your chosen Attention Cue, just after his name, before he looks in your eyes. Do not repeat it over and over if you get no response. Just wait and mark once you do get the desired response.
- Don't worry about requiring your dog to sit for this at first. It will become automatic with practice. The most important thing is that he looks in your eyes, even if it is brief.
- Capture the moment! You may think that your dog isn't looking at you or he isn't looking long enough to be rewarded. He is, just perfect your timing and you will increase the duration of the behavior. Just a quick glance into your eyes is enough to get started – be sure to capture it.
- Happy voices invite your dog to want to look at you. Be your dog's party. Dogs like to have fun!
- If your dog is looking at you before you even say your Attention Cue, mark the moment with your marker word at the exact moment he looks at you, regardless of whether you got to say your word yet. Wait until he turns his head and use your word then.
- The timing of the Marker Word is more important than the timing of the treat. The Marker Word needs to be said at the EXACT moment that your dog looks into your eyes. The treat should follow as soon as possible, but your hands will never be as fast as your mouth can be!
- Make sure that you are not offering the treat when your dog is jumping or something else that is not desirable, but don't fret over making the treat happen at the same time as the Attention Cue.
- Any uninitiated looks into your eyes should be equally marked with an enthusiastic Marker Word as well. The ultimate object of this Attention Cue is to teach your dog to look to you for information, both on his own and when invited to.
- All family members should practice this exercise.

- You can easily practice this at random times throughout the day, such as when you are preparing dinner, during commercial breaks while you are watching TV, when you are preparing for work or bed, etc. Make it a routine part of your day.
- Once you have perfected the Attention Cue inside your home, take it outside in your yard. Work on that for several weeks and then and only then should you try it on walks. Start with low distraction walks at first. Move forward in baby steps. Set your dog up for success!

WHEN TO USE THIS:

- When you need to regain your dog's attention from something very interesting. (bicycle, squirrel, cat, jogger, another dog, etc.)
- Before your dog spots something he may find fascinating, to keep his attention on you!
- To teach him to frequently check in with you.
- To reinforce that you are available to handle all things that come up.
- To reinforce that all relevant information comes from you!

Real Life Attention Cue

JEN USES "LOOK" AS HER ATTENTION CUE. *When she is trying to get her crew to look at her for taking pictures, she gets a fast response with a "Look". She also uses this cue when they are playing and the dogs miss where the ball went. When they respond to the "Look" cue, she then directs them to where the toy is and play resumes!*

LILIAN REGULARLY WALKS HER DOGS *all at once in a very distracting urban environment. She uses "Look" to get them to look at her during walks. Usually her dogs stop what they are doing and glance at her immediately. If they think a treat is coming, they will even come and sit in front of her. This helps her to keep the focus on her rather than the busy environment. She also uses her "Look" cue before she asks them to come to her. This helps to keep her recall cue much more reliable by getting her dog's attention first.*

GO TO MAT

   This next cue has multiple uses. It can teach your dog that his mat is a portable safe place. You can take his mat anywhere and it is an island in chaos. It is also the perfect cue for use during the human mealtime. See how many uses you can find for this cue. This cue was written by me with inspiration from a couple of trainers who taught this to me. Thanks, Sheri and Leslie!

OBJECT: To teach your dog to go to a specific place such as a portable mat.

INSTRUCTION:
1. Get a towel or a flat dog bed or mat of some kind (Target has excellent inexpensive ones, make sure you use a flat, NOT fluffy one) and act VERY interested in it. Make sure that your dog sees you do this. Place the mat on the floor near you. As soon as your dog shows an interest in it at all such as sniffing it, walking on it, looking at it, pawing it, etc. click or say "yes!" and place a treat right ON THE MAT (do not give the treat to your dog by your hand).
2. As long as your dog keeps showing interest in any way with the mat, click/mark the behavior and toss the treat ON THE MAT. ANY behavior that you get while the dog is on the mat is clickable.
3. You will begin using two levels of treats once your dog is staying on the mat and offering any behaviors (sit, down, etc.). You can use either more of a certain treat or a higher value treat, when your dog offers a "down" as opposed to other offerings. That will show your dog that anything done on the mat is a good thing but a "down" gets the best stuff!
4. Once your dog is offering a "down" reliably, then use your release word and call him off the mat if need be. Use your party voice and make it fun, as any recall should be. But in this instance, do not treat your dog for coming off the mat. The release word will always signify the end of a behavior. You want the rewards to happen during any behavior, not after.
5. After your dog comes off the mat and you have acknowledged that, stand perfectly still and wait for your dog to show interest

in the mat again. Once he does, resume step #3. Make sure it is very clear that it is being on the mat that causes the rewards to come. Once you get reliable downs again, go to step #4 again.

6. When your dog is showing a clear preference for staying on the mat, start increasing the time between rewards. If he vacates the mat before you release him, pick up the mat briefly and ignore him. Then make a big show of getting the mat and trying again. Once he is remaining on the mat until you issue a release cue, then start walking around the mat in a circle. Go in small steps according to your own dog's personality. Some dogs will be too upset or excited if you move fast and some will be fine. Know your dog. After each step away without a release cue, return quickly (but without much movement on your part) and drop another treat on the mat. It is important that your dog understand that the treats come ONLY on the mat, whether you step away or not.

7. Once you reach the point that your dog is staying on the mat until you issue a release cue, even if you have stepped away quite far, you can then name this behavior. When you can, then pick up the mat and place it back down and say your desired name cue just as you are laying it down. Then click/ mark the behavior. You will need several successions in order to associate the name with the behavior, but it will become clear with repetition. Name it whatever you want! Be creative. Go to Place, Go to Mat, Where's Your Bed, Chill Out, etc. It only needs to mean something to you and your dog.

8. You should also leave your mat out as often as you can and reward your dog for choosing to lie on it. If your dog goes to the mat of his own volition, then he is free to come and go from the mat as he chooses. If you cue him to GO TO MAT, then you must be the one to release him from the mat.

9. While in every other aspect of your life with your dog, the treats should come directly from you, the mat is different. It is the magic mat. Any behavior done on the mat, requires that the treat be given by dropping it ON THE MAT! Make the mat magic.

Real Life Go to Mat

LILIAN'S DOGS SOMETIMES THINK *that every time she moves around in the evening that it means they can go outside yet again. If their needs are all met and she just wants to relax for a bit, she cues them to "Go Lie Down". Her dogs have been taught that this means go to a dog bed and lay down. Instant relaxing time!*

JOYCE'S ROTTWEILER MIX KENDRA LOVES PEOPLE, *but sometimes she gets a little over-exuberant with visitors. If this occurs, she gets told to "Go to Your Mat." Once she's calmed down on her mat, she gets released to visit again. If she again gets too pushy for attention, or tries to lick the visitors to death, she gets sent her to her mat again until she once again settles down. She's learned to better control herself around visitors, knowing that if she doesn't, she spends more time on her mat than greeting friends!*

WAIT

Now we come to one of the handiest cues that you can have in a multiple dog household. The "wait" cue has a multitude of uses. You can use this on walks, when you go from one room to the next and you'd like to do it without all the dogs, when you have the dogs accompany you on vehicle errands, when you want them to go out the door when YOU say so, the list is endless.

OBJECT: To teach your dog to hang around where you leave him and wait for further instructions before going elsewhere. WAIT does not require your dog to maintain the exact position, but he cannot follow you or move far away. WAIT requires further instruction or your return.

INSTRUCTION:
- This cue has many uses so be patient while teaching this cue as it requires time so that your dog will eventually generalize the word to each situation that you use it. But once he does, it sure is handy!

- The best way to start using this cue is to teach a "WAIT" at the door, which requires you to give another cue to allow your dog to go further.
- Position your dog at the door and while slowly opening the door, say "WAIT". If he moves towards the door at all, close the door. You will need to set aside a period of time to do this, it may not happen in moments. You are actually using going out of the door as the reward. While your dog waits patiently rather than rushing the door, you may mark it with a "YES" but in this instance, it should be a happy but quieter yes than you are used to so as to not excite your dog. Once you get the door completely opened, quickly release him after saying a happy "YES!" Do not keep asking your dog to sit or wait. Just wait until he offers a sit or stops going forward to start opening the door "very" slowly once again. He will get it.
- Another instance for the WAIT cue is when you are walking your dog and need to stop and do something such as tie your shoe or navigate a street crossing. Instruct your dog to "WAIT" and reward heavily with praise while you are tying your shoe or waiting for the traffic to thin. Make sure you issue the release cue when it is time to move again. If your dog moves around so much that there is tension on the leash, you may use a verbal interrupter such as "Ah-Ah" to get his attention (keep this to a minimum) or simply hold on very tight and wait for the second that the tension abates. Once he moves back into your space enough to release the tension on the leash, reward with praise and resume your actions until you need to release him to move once again.
- This cue can also be used in instances where you take your dog with you on errands in the car. You obviously do not want him to maintain a structured sit for this but you want him to understand that he is staying in the vehicle. You can do this similarly to the method used for the door exercise. Make sure that he is not too close to the door when you open it and use your "Ah-Ah" sound if needed. I try and restrict that sound to safety issues.
- Reward for not trying to rush the door. In this instance, the eventual reward is your return and praise for being there. Be lavish with praise. It makes a difference.

- For in-home situations, this cue is also ideal for times that you don't want your dog to follow you, such as when you are watching tv and you get up to go in another room and intend to return shortly. You use the "WAIT" cue here. Make sure to praise lavishly for remaining where you left him.

Real Life Wait

LILIAN USES "WAIT" FOR HER DOGS *when they get out of the car. She does not want her dogs jumping out of doors as soon as they are opened. She prefers that they wait until she tells them it's time to jump out of the car. So, when she opens the door, she says their names individually and tells them to "Wait." She then individually releases each one of them one at a time to jump out of the car.*

JEN USES "WAIT" MOST FREQUENTLY *when letting her dogs outside. She has tie outs in her unfenced yard. She and Jeff bring the dogs out on to the back porch, and they get told to "Wait" until they are clipped onto their long line. If one of them gets out of the door without having a hold on their collar, a "Wait" keeps them safely on the porch until the leashing is completed. They are released with a cue once they are fully leashed.*

CRYSTAL ALSO HAS MULTIPLE USES *for the "Wait" cue. Even though she has a fenced-in back yard and doesn't need to take the dogs out on leashes, she and Ross use "Wait" before opening the back door so that the dogs don't charge past them. They release the dogs one at a time to reduce chaos. It makes for much less potential destruction when all the dogs are eager for their morning potty trip! She also finds "Wait" to be very helpful when trying to transfer things from inside the house to outside or vice versa, with the dogs looking eagerly at an open door. Other scenarios where she has made good use of this cue include when opening the back of her SUV to keep the dogs from trying to exit while harnessed in, when opening crate doors and even at bedtime, when they ask the dogs to wait on the floor until they allow them up into bed with them.*

DROP IT

Now we come to the "drop it" cue, which is handy for any food/treat situation and is also important on walks, especially if you live in the city. This was originally written by Lilian Akin of Akin Family Dog Training in Pittsburgh, PA and it was revised by me for my style and preferences.

OBJECT: To teach your dog how to drop anything in his mouth when given a cue. You can name this anything you want. "drop it, "give", etc.

INSTRUCTION:
1. Give your dog something that he is likely to take into his mouth such as a rawhide, stick, ball or favored toy.
   - It should be something big enough for you to grab hold of on one end.
   - Have HIGH VALUE treats ready in the other hand. Show them to your dog.
   - As you offer the object that you want your dog to take, you can say the words **"TAKE IT"** if you are also interested in this cue. His reward for this cue is to be able to take the object in his mouth. Say "yes!" when he does this. If you are not interested in this cue, simply skip that part and wait until your dog holds onto the object, even slightly.
2. After your dog has taken the object in his mouth, *gently* hold the end of the object and say your cue word. ("**DROP IT**") (If your dog guards, do NOT hold the object. Simply show the treats and offer a trade. Reward HEAVILY with the high value treats if he drops the object. If you are holding onto the object, mark even the lessening of pressure from your dog's mouth. Say "yes!" and offer a treat for this. Repeat.
   - Do not hold onto the object hard or pull on it at all.
   - Simply place enough gentle pressure on the object to retain a hold on it.
   - You want your dog to voluntarily release tension on the object; you are not trying to pull it from his mouth.
   - If you pull too hard, you will start a tug of war game. If this happens, your dog is unlikely to let go. Just walk away. Don't acknowledge this at all, just walk away for thirty

seconds or so and try again.

- If your dog does not drop the object for the treat, you might need to find a tastier treat. Use something your dog loves more than the object in his mouth. Think VERY high value, such as boiled chicken.

3. Repeat steps 1 and 2. Practice some form of object exchange (exchanging a rawhide, stick, or toy for a treat) every day, multiple times a day. This is very important as it could save your dog's life in the future.

4. Once your dog readily takes and drops objects, you can stop using treats 100% of the time. Your dog's reward can often be continuation of the game, if you are using a toy at practice. This means that he knows that he almost always gets the toy back. Randomly use treats so there is always a higher incentive attached to "drop it".

5. Offer a food reward when your dog relinquishes something he really wants, in a real life situation.

TIPS:

- Practice this over and over with your dog. The more you practice this cue and make it like a game, the more automatic your dog's "drop" behavior will become.

- If your dog has a positive experience every time you practice this exercise with him, the more likely he is to willingly drop something dangerous he picks up, such as a cooked chicken bone or chocolate.

- It is ok to play tug of war with your dog as long as you play by your rules and your dog willingly takes and drops the object on cue.

- Be sure to use time outs in response to any inappropriate behavior during a game of tug. Example: if his teeth ever touch your body during the game, simply stop playing and walk away for a minute. Don't say anything, don't chastise. Just walk away. Then come back and continue playing. Repeat the time out if you feel teeth. If the teeth continue after three tries, the toy gets put away.

Real Life Drop It

LILIAN HAS HAD AN EXCITING EXPERIENCE where the "Drop It" cue *came in very handy. She was walking her dogs and a loose Yorkie came running out at them from a front yard. He was off leash and her three dogs were on leash. He circled them, all the while barking and lunging at them. Her Greyhound Phoenix picked him up and she immediately cued him to "Drop It" and he spit him out. The Yorkie ran back to his owner unhurt and a bit wiser!*

CHRIS USES "DROP IT" WITH APACHE. *He loves to steal things from Cherokee or Alexandra (the human baby!) so when he does, she tells him to "Drop It". He always does now and he gets lots of praise each time!*

JOYCE'S BORDER COLLIE MIX BAXTER *is a retrieving fanatic. He particularly loves to catch a flying disc, and although he always drops it when he brings it back, she got tired of bending over to pick it up. So she shaped the simple "Drop It" into a more complex "Bring" where he places the disc into her hand. She did this at first by stooping over and putting her hands under the disc before he dropped it. If he missed, he had to try again. Once he got the idea that she'd throw it again only if he dropped in into her hands, she gradually bent over less until she was standing upright. She also gradually reduced how far she extended her hands. Now he brings his disc back and slaps it right into her hand for another throw and her back feels much better!*

LEAVE IT

The next cue we will cover is actually the predecessor to the "drop it" cue. The "leave it" is used before the dog picks up the object that you don't want him to have. Aim to use this more than a "drop it" This cue was also originally written by Lilian Akin and revised by me.

OBJECT: To teach your dog to ignore something he finds really interesting when told to "**LEAVE IT.**"

INSTRUCTION:

1. Take a really high-value treat in one hand and show it to your dog.
   - Have more treats in your other hand ready to offer as a reward but don't show the treats to your dog yet. Put that hand behind your back.
2. As your dog approaches or looks at the treat in your offered hand, tell your dog to *"***LEAVE IT.***"*
   - If your dog licks and paws at your hand to try and get the treats, don't say anything, just wait for him to stop.
   - The second your dog stops trying to get the treat or looks or backs away from the treat say **"YES"** and offer a treat from your hidden hand. Be sure to reward your dog verbally for a job well done.
   - Repeat this step over and over again until your dog appears to understand that **"LEAVE IT"** means to ignore the treat in your hand. Be sure to switch hands and mix up what hand you use for the temptation as well as the reward.
3. For the next step, take the high value treat and put it in front of your dog on the floor. Cover it partially with your hand or foot so that he cannot get it.
   - As your dog approaches or looks at the treat, tell your dog to "**LEAVE IT**."
   - The second your dog stops trying to get the treat or looks away or backs up from the treat say **"YES"** and offer a treat from your hand. Be sure to reward your dog verbally for a job well done.
   - Repeat this step over and over again until your dog appears to understand that **"LEAVE IT"** means to ignore the treat on the floor.
   - As your dog gets better at not trying to get the treat on the floor, you can make it harder by leaving the treat more open. But take this in slow steps. Set your dog up for success!
4. When you are done practicing, offer your dog the tasty treat with which you have been practicing. Always give it to him personally by hand rather than releasing him to take it from the floor. This reinforces that all good things come from you!

5. Place a high value treat or bowl of food on the floor. Have treats ready in your hand to offer as a reward.
   - Practice walking your dog (on a short leash) around the treat/food, while not giving him enough leash to actually reach the treat or bowl. When your dog shows interest by looking or lunging at the treat/food, tell your dog "**LEAVE IT**" and wait for him to stop trying to get it or better yet, look away from it and/or at you. Do not use a leash jerk to gain his attention. Simply keep him far enough away from the desired item that he cannot reach it. Use your voice to get his attention. Keeping your dog moving away from the object, rather than standing near it, helps this process move faster.
   - The second your dog looks away from the treat or bowl, even if it's very slightly, say "**YES**" and offer a treat. Be sure to reward your dog verbally for a job well done.
6. Try tossing a treat or a piece of kibble on the floor right in front of your dog so that he sees it.
   - When your dog shows interest by looking or lunging at the treat, tell your dog "**LEAVE IT**".
   - The second your dog looks away from the treat or kibble say "**YES**" and offer a treat. Be sure to also reward your dog verbally for a job well done.

Real Life Leave It

LILIAN USED "LEAVE IT" when she first adopted her Greyhound straight from the track. He had been cat tested, but she was worried about his reaction to a house full of cats who run. So, she worked very hard on teaching him a really positive "Leave It." This meant that he would leave whatever he was interested in and come to her for a really good reward. Soon anytime he saw a cat, he would come running to her without even being told to "Leave It." Lilian also uses "Leave it" to keep the peace at mealtimes. Her dogs love to check out each other's meal areas and to see if there is anything left to lick from the floor or the bowls. She uses "Leave It" to prevent fights at meal times.

JEN USES "LEAVE IT" when food items have been accidentally

dropped on the floor. Takoda comes running, but she tells him to "Leave it" and he will not go near whatever has fallen.

CHRIS USES "LEAVE IT" *with her crew when they see things like dead (or even live) animals and the like that she doesn't want them to bother with. Cherokee loves snakes. They have a lot of garter snakes where they live so she is constantly trying to sniff them. A "Leave It" helps her ignore them.*

WHEN CRYSTAL'S DOGS EAT, *her picky eater Sammy generally needs some coercion in the form of watered down canned food or perhaps a little boiled venison in order to convince him to eat his prescription diet food. Because his food generally smells extra special to the other dogs, they would have a big mess on their hands if they didn't teach everyone the cue "Leave It!" Everyone understands that they must stay away from Sammy's food, but if a wandering nose brings them too close to his dinner, this cue is all it takes to remind them to mind their own business. This, combined with a down-stay when needed, keeps the disorder out of mealtimes for them.*

JUMPING

Solving jumping issues does not use a step-by-step procedure, but it is one of the most common behavior issues.

The reasons behind jumping are many and include friendly greetings, anticipation, attention seeking, etc. Your response to your dog's jumping will determine how quickly you can redirect his behavior into something much more preferable. Redirecting jumping behavior can seem like an endless commitment to work, but with consistency on your part, it will get better!

Greeting jumping:

Stand up straight and do not use your hands to push your dog away. Using your hands will be seen as an interactive game to your dog and is as rewarding as the jumping itself.

Use your body to claim your space. Step slightly forward and turn around at the same time, ending up with your back to your dog. Do not acknowledge the jumping. Wait until your dog sits and mark that moment with a "YES!" and then offer a treat.

Do not hold the treat up high and entice your dog to jump again. It's better if the treats are completely hidden. The dog only gets the treat if he remains in the seated position. This then teaches your dog to do a default sit and also that sitting will get him positive attention in multiple situations.

If you work hard enough at teaching your dog that a sit is always appropriate if he is confused, he will always default to it. You can then say "SIT!" when he is jumping and have him slam his butt to the floor rather than jumping. If the jumping continues even with your back turned, to an alarming degree, employ a Time Out (see Time Out instructions). Return to Jumping redirection training once the Time Out has accomplished its purpose.

Getting your guests to go along with your desire to keep your dog from jumping will not always be easy. Keep a bowl of tasty treats by the door when you are expecting guests. Explaining to your guests what you are trying to accomplish and asking for their help will go farther than just telling your dog not to jump on them. Many people will say that they don't mind and will pet your dog while he is jumping. This, of course, reinforces the jumping and that is definitely not what you want.

Ask your guests to only acknowledge your dog when he is NOT jumping and make sure they understand the method that you are using to redirect this behavior. Emphasize the treat portion of the method. Giving treats is something that most people enjoy doing for dogs so your guests get a reward for assisting with the training too! If you have guests whom you know will not comply with this or you have service people working in your home, simply put your dog in another room with an interesting diversion rather than be inconsistent with his training.

You can also set up jumping training by placing your dog on a leash and either tethering him to something or having someone hold onto the leash. Walk towards your dog and if he jumps, immediately stop your forward movement. When he either stands with all four paws on the floor or sits, then proceed forward towards him once again. If he jumps back up, stop again. Repeat this process as often as possible. It's better to not say anything than to acknowledge the jumping.

CRATE TRAINING

With some dogs, you can simply place them in the crate with a Kong® and all will be well with the world. With other dogs, you could have a mess on your hands when you get home if this were how you handled your dog's first experience with a crate. Most dogs fall somewhere in between. The key to having your dog accept the crate, if he has not been crate trained as a puppy, is to make the crate the most positive experience that you possibly can. You will do this in steps.

Begin by assembling the crate in an area that you are used to spending time with your dog in. One of the biggest mistakes that dog owners make is placing the crate in a little used area, such as a basement or laundry room. Sure, it's out of the way and not an eyesore there, but it's also banishment in the eyes of your dog. Actually, it's double banishment. Why? Your dog's favorite human is gone and he cannot pass the time waiting for your return in his favorite spot, but must instead be in lockdown in an area that has no positive memories for him! It doesn't get much more upsetting than that.

So if you are that concerned with how the crate looks in your home, then get one of the fancier ones that are available that look like furniture or artwork.

Chances are that unless you have brought all of your dogs into your home at the same time (and you shouldn't do this!), then you will not be crating all of your dogs at once. If you have gotten to this chapter, then you will probably have already read the tips on crating multiple dogs safely. This portion here is simply for instructing you on how to make the crate a happy place: so back to the program at hand.

Once you have the crate assembled, place VERY high value treats inside and don't show your dog who you are training to like the crate that you have done this. Let him find them. If you are only acclimating one dog to the crate at this time, then you must supply the other dogs with some recreation in another area of the house to prevent interruption. Once your trainee finds the treats, while he is still inside the crate, murmur that he is a good boy and act pleased about this development. The next time you set this up, you could place a filled Kong® inside. Another idea is to rub a bit of peanut butter on a few of the back bars of the crate so that the only way to get the reward is by being inside of the crate.

The first few times your dog finds the high value treat or the filled Kong®, he may bring it out of the crate to eat it. That is fine. There will come a time where he will eat it inside of the crate standing up and then again, a more exciting time when he lies down to eat it inside of the crate. Note this verbally when he is involved in eating, but note it quietly so as to not startle him into coming out.

Once you have him staying in there at times of his own volition while he eats, close the crate door and stay in the room. Open it before he is done eating but only just before. Act very casual. Slowly increase the time frames that you have the crate door closed. Then begin briefly leaving the room when the crate door is closed, always when your dog is eating. You can then progress to leaving the house briefly at first.

You may wonder how you can possibly leave the house and keep your dog and your house safe while you are slowly desensitizing your dog to the crate. As long as your dog is not harming himself in the crate while he is in there, you are simply crating him anyway. But in the meantime, you are making this more pleasant by the day so it will cause you both less stress.

If on the other hand, your dog is injuring himself while crated, then you need professional assistance. Get that for your dog as fast as you can. I can't teach that in a book. It's an individualized process based on your dog's needs.

Some options until you are able to get a behavioral intervention are doggy daycare and/or a petsitter. Pricey but worth it for your dog's sanity.

But back to crate training. Once you have started leaving the crate door closed successfully and are now leaving the house even briefly, the true key to making the crate a happy place is to replicate the environment of when you are home. Play a radio or a tv station that your dog is used to hearing, provided it's a calming sound. No heavy metal at loud volumes, please! If your dog reacts at certain sounds or sights on a tv and you are watching something that may contain something reaction causing, then switch the channel before you leave.

Another important thing to note is that the room that contains the crate should not be the room that is nearest to outside activity. This can cause more distress in your dog than is advised when you are not home and he is feeling vulnerable.

Some dogs do better in a covered crate and some want to see what is coming at them. You will have to learn what is best for your dog. Many a dog who is distressed when alone, will shred some item in the crate if you give him the opportunity. So don't go there. This can include a crate cover.

Plan to use items in the crate that are safe for your dog to use when unsupervised. These items include the Kong® (if your dog is not among those who can ingest one!), hard Nylabones®, most uncooked marrow bones and some interactive toys. As advised in a previous chapter, the key to safe unsupervised toys is to know your dog's chewing style and what he can and cannot chew up.

Where bedding is concerned, your dog does not need a soft surface in his crate if he is simply going to chew it up. If he doesn't chew soft items, you can certainly provide him with bedding.

He also does not need water that he will almost certainly spill. Too much food provided to a crated dog can create the need to eliminate when there is no way for him to get out to do so. You will then have a very frustrated and anxious dog. So please be sure to make thoroughly pottying your dog the last thing that you do before crating him.

I am a thorough believer in not crating a dog for longer than a five hour stretch. If you are like most people and you work an 8 hour shift away from home, then you will need to get creative. Your dog is definitely not going to welcome crating when it happens for un-reasonable time periods! One option is a petsitter or dog walker. If this is cost prohibitive, then perhaps neighbors or close by relatives are an option? You will be pleasantly surprised at just how much of a calming difference a mid-crating break can mean to your dog. Having this break to look forward to can help your dog to cope with the stress that being crated can cause him. If you by some chance live close to your place of employment, then coming home briefly can offer respite.

In a previous chapter, several calming remedies were discussed.

Crating is another perfect opportunity to put these products to excellent use. Spraying Comfort Zone® on bedding in the crate or on fabrics near the crate can help keep your dog calm. If you have the crate in a smallish room that is not in an open floor plan, using the plug in version of Comfort Zone® would be ideal. Dosing your dog with Rescue Remedy® approximately fifteen minutes prior to leaving would be very helpful. Be mindful that Rescue Remedy® really only has about a two hour window so it will not be responsible for calming your dog for longer crated periods, but it will certainly help with the transition from you being home to you leaving. Another useful product in this circumstance is Chill Out. I spray this throughout my bedroom before I leave my dogs. It has made a huge difference with Trent when he is left alone while the other dogs are being walked. He no longer chews items that are not meant to be chewed since I began using this.

Being matter of fact when you leave the house will also make a difference. Acting guilty and worried when you leave will give the impression to your dog that he has a reason to worry. So don't make a fuss, either when you leave or when you return. I have a key phrase that I say to my dogs prior to leaving. It seems to let them know that all is well and that I will return. Develop a phrase if it helps you and your dogs to transition better.

Being patient with your dog will help this go more smoothly. Remembering to make the crate a safe-feeling and happy place will ensure that your dog's crating experience is the best it can be and that is good for both you and your dogs!

Graduating from the crate:

You will almost certainly want to wean your dogs away from the crate. That's fine. But do remember that multiple dogs behave like multiple dogs at times. This means that a pack mentality can ensue. Please make sure that each of your precious pups is gradually introduced to more freedom on an individual basis so that manners will be the collective thought process rather than mayhem.

Whenever it's time to go to the next level after the crate, the best option is to give freedom in increments. Baby gate your sophomore in a restricted area that is as dog proofed as you can get it, along with the usual accoutrements for a home alone pup such a Kong® and the like.

Can the restricted area be near the rest of the crew? Yes, with a caveat. If you are at all worried about how the formerly crated one and any other crew member may get along when unsupervised, then not yet would be the answer. Take no chances where safety is concerned.

Once your newly uncrated pup proves his worth in this restricted area, you can experiment with a larger area of freedom. Exploring this in slowly increasing increments is your best prospect for success. Going slowly is building a sturdy foundation, to better guarantee safety and success. If you have a slip up, simply go back a step and decrease the freedom for a bit. Then repeat. Success is in your pup's future if you proceed in this manner!

Real Life Crate Training

LILIAN ALWAYS HAS ANY NEW DOG CRATED, *usually in the living or dining room; until she is sure the newbie understands the rules of the house, gets along with the other dogs and the cats, is housetrained and is not going to chew anything inappropriate. She initially crated JJ for about six months. He was six months when she rescued him and she graduated him from the crate when he was about a year old. She crated her Greyhound for about a month and a half when she adopted him from the track. She always crates foster dogs who are visitors to her home.*

CRYSTAL IS OF THE OPINION THAT CRATES ARE NECESSARY *in a house with multiple dogs. She uses them often enough that she rarely has to apply a cue anymore; the dogs in her home simply run to the crate doors and wait to be let in. Toby will even open his door if it's not latched, and let himself in! It's a comforting place for the dogs to go so they frequently give the dogs a break in their crates with a yummy Kong or a raw bone so they can relax. They sometimes use the crates to separate dogs for mealtimes until they understand how to down-stay for their supper or if they have any food related issues, even sometimes just for the slow eaters so they can take their time and feel comfortable. They also use crates for dogs who would get into trouble when they cannot be directly supervised or even when the people or dogs in their house just need time away from one another for a while! They have also been known to use crates in the car when carrying multiple dogs so they can't get their harnesses and tethers tangled or possibly injure one another.*

RECALLS

And now we come to the recall instructions. This could be one of the most important things that you teach your dog. This is another cue that was initially written by Lilian Akin and revised by me.

OBJECTIVE: To teach you how to have your dog come quickly to you when requested.

INSTRUCTION:
- You can begin this exercise by having someone hold your dog while you walk away from him. If no helper is available, try working with your dog inside the house or in a distraction-free environment. Never put your dog into a stay and call him out of it to come to you. If you use a word to keep him where he is, use "wait".
- Say your dog's name in the happiest sounding voice you can muster. Once his head turns towards you, say "yes!" or click and go in the opposite direction from him, all the while using your voice to encourage him towards you. At first, you will not use a word for this such as "Come". You will get him to do this reliably a few times and once he is doing well at it, you will say the word you want to mean "come to me right now" after his name, just as he begins moving towards you.
- When your dog reaches you, count to fifteen while interacting with him heavily, including giving him HIGH value treats, petting, verbal rewards and even a bit of rough play if that is what he enjoys. Make this encounter memorable. Make him think that coming to you is the best thing since sliced liver!
- Make every encounter that your dog chooses to have with you a good one. Reward him for random checking in, both inside the house and out, especially on walks. Make hanging by you more fun than anything else.

TIPS

- **NEVER PUNISH YOUR DOG FOR COMING TO YOU or CALL YOUR DOG TO YOU TO PUNISH HIM NO MATTER HOW ANGRY YOU ARE AT HIM!** If you punish your dog for not coming or call your dog to you to punish him, he will begin to fear coming, because he connects coming to you with punishment. Instead, don't punish at all and make coming to you the best thing ever.

- Avoid calling your dog to you if you must do something that he perceives as unpleasant, such as giving him a pill, putting him in the crate, giving him a bath, ending a play session, etc. If you must do something that he perceives as unpleasant, just go get him.

- If your dog has learned to ignore you when you give the "COME" cue, you should think about re-naming the cue to something like "FRONT" or "HERE." Start over with a completely new cue. Make one up. Remember, it only need make sense to you and your dog.

- Make coming to you when called the most wonderful thing in your dog's life. It could save your dog's life some day.

- Avoid using your leash to pull your dog to you or to tug on his leash when asking him to come. You want your dog to make the decision to come to you on his own. You also don't want your dog to be dependent upon the leash tug; otherwise he won't come to you when off leash.

- Practice this exercise on and off leash.

- Practice this exercise in many different locations, including in the house. Play hide and seek in the house and make it a party when he finds you! This can be especially fun if you have multiple family members play along at the same time.

- If using treats or a toy or something that motivates your dog, try not to show it to him when you call him (unless you still need to go get your dog to lure him to you.) It is fine to use treats/toys as lures initially, but repeated and on-going use of a lure will fail more often than not. If your dog sees in advance that you are holding something to reward him in exchange for a behavior, he can then weigh its value against whatever it is he would rather be doing. Instead, make the rewards for coming when called interesting, exciting, and unpredictable.

Treats as rewards are far better than lures in certain behaviors and if he never knows when he is getting a reward or what kind, you then become a human slot machine, which is extremely attractive to your dog!

Real Life Recalls

WHEN JOYCE TAKES HER CREW TO THE PARK, *they get some off leash time so good recalls are vital. She always carries two different kinds of treats in this scenario: a dry biscuit-type cookie, and something really tasty, like chicken, roast beef, hot dogs, cheese, etc. When her dogs come running back to her on their own for a "check in", they get a cookie. When she calls them to come, they get the good stuff! So they are encouraged and rewarded both for coming back on their own for a "check in", and for coming promptly when called. She'll also often reward a recall by simply sending the dog off to play again, so that coming to her does not mean that playtime is over. Joyce also has a little trick she uses when she encounters people with no control over their off leash dogs. She has taught her dogs an extra recall cue: when she shouts "Call your dog please!" or "Get your dog!", her dogs now think these phrases means "come to mom for super yummy treats!" What a great idea!*

CRYSTAL FEELS THAT RECALLS ARE IMPORTANT *in her home for keeping peace and order within her crew of dogs. The most common need she has in her home for a recall is distracting a dog from whatever he happens to be doing. For instance, the yard is great fun for everyone but occasionally the dogs bark at things going on outside the fence perimeter. To help preserve the sanity of their neighbors before all the dogs join forces, they've learned how to maximize the time it takes to call all of them at once by teaching a solid recall that everyone understands. She does mention that they do make sure to get out of the way when they issue a group recall as they don't want to be run down in the stampede! Recalls also work well for head counts, as when they sometimes have as many as eight dogs wandering around the yard or house, it's easy* to lose track. Finally, Crystal notes that lore says two heads are better than one, and for dogs, the more the merrier when it comes to things like plotting an escape or getting into trouble. When dogs "help" each other dig out of a fence or find a hole in it, it's more crucial than ever to be able to call them back. This has happened to them on two occasions and without the time they have spent teaching a solid recall, their dogs could have been in all the more danger.

LOOSE LEASH WALKING

The next instruction that we have is about loose leash walking. Another tough behavior to teach but not impossible. Patience is really important when teaching this. Some of this instruction was originally written by a colleague named Barb Grosch and later expanded and revised by me.

Teaching your dog how to walk on a loose leash is one of the hardest cues to teach, because each time your dog pulls you and gets to go forward, he is being rewarded for pulling you. So the hardest part for you as the owner is to resist going forward until your dog has the idea that tension on the leash is a no-no. The following pointers should help your dog learn to walk nicely without pulling. Some of these can be used together and some are meant as alternatives.

- If your dog pulls on the leash during a walk, stop dead in your tracks. Do not yank on the leash or even say anything. Wait for the tension to loosen up on the leash before you continue to walk forward. Waiting until your dog turns and looks at you can work even better and it creates a bond, while reminding him that someone is holding that end of the leash.
- Get your dog's attention before starting to walk. A dog that is looking at you while you walk cannot be pulling you. Make it fun to look at you.
- If your dog pulls, back up a few steps. Do not yank your dog, but guide him with the leash or lure him with treats into the walk position. Once your dog is by your side, resume walking.

He is penalized for pulling by losing ground.
- Try quick turns and circles to keep your dog looking at you. He must pay attention to the unpredictable human on the other end of the leash. Do not use a jerking motion on the leash to get him to come with you. Use a very happy voice and make it a party!
- Try stopping and having your dog sit frequently during the walk. That reminds him that someone is holding the leash!
- Try using a treat or toy to lure your dog into the walk position by your side. Do not use the food as a bribe but only as a lure and/or reward.
- Talk to your dog to keep his attention and to engage him. Use happy tones. Again, think party!
- Use your marker word (yes!) and rewards (treats, etc.) to reward loose leash walking. IE: When your dog chooses to walk next to you or even just on a loose leash, not pulling, say "yes!" and offer him a treat.
- Try to keep the treats hidden so that your dog is not just staying by you for the food. Make it about the bond.
- When you jerk on the leash, it generally causes dog to pull harder right back. This is called the "opposition reflex" and it's a natural reflex but not a desirable one.

The sure way to train your dog to loose leash walk in approximately two weeks, is to make sure that each and every time he pulls, you do not go forward. Doing so will reward him for pulling and we all know that repetition of rewards is what causes a dog to strive for what he wants. In order to do this successfully, you will need to differentiate between training walks and managed walks. Managed walks will be done using some sort of management device such as a front clip harness, etc., so that you can have a stress free walk and still remain upright. Your training during these walks will be more minimal than without it.

On the training walks, you will employ any or all of the above methods, in order that your dog fully understands that pulling will get him no where. It may take you a half-hour to get to the end of the block, but the message will be crystal clear! Pull and go no where. If you are a small person and you have a large dog, pulling may inadvertently move you despite your desired resistance. Your best bet is to get yourself a waist belt leash so that you can have extra leverage to be able to resist the pull. Never yank on the leash or pull back. Simple resistance to forward movement will get the point across.

The key to making your message clear is to move forward as fast as you can when there is no tension on the leash, until the leash is taut, when you will again go back to your training methods above. It must be clear that the only way to proceed forward is a loose leash. With consistency, your dog will soon learn the difference and you should be able to take walks without a management device most of the time! Practice makes perfect!

One thing that I recommend practicing frequently is loose leash walking at home, without a leash. Make it fun to walk by your side and your dog will have a history that he can refer back to when on a leash. Start in the house and work up to practicing in your yard, if it is fenced. Follow the above procedure for actual leash walks and in no time, you will have a smooth walk to look forward to.

Real Life Loose Leash Walking

CRYSTAL IS CONVINCED THAT HER DOGS *used to seem to think they were training for the Iditarod. She worked individually on loose leash manners until she felt that each dog knew what was expected of him or her. The day she was able to walk three of them home from a hike in a heel pattern beside her felt great!*

JOYCE HAS FOUND TEACHING LOOSE LEASH WALKING *more difficult with some dogs than with others, but with consistency and yummy rewards they've all learned. She uses plenty of rewards when a dog is just learning, and gradually fades the number of treats that she gives as they get better at it. Once walking nicely becomes a habit, she rewards them by occasionally telling them to "go play" and letting them walk to the end of their retractable leash when they're in an appropriate area like the park. Even then, she says that they don't pull. They usually wander back to her side after a few minutes in front of her - because they have found that to be the most rewarding place to be!*

EFFECTIVE TIME OUTS

Although this is not a step-by-step training cue, this has always been very helpful for my clients. Time outs can give your dog important information.

Time outs are very important tools to advise your dog when he has done something you would prefer he not do. A time out consists of removing your attention from your dog, which is often the most important thing in the world to him.

There are two types of time outs. You can either withdraw your attention from your dog by turning your back on him or going into a closed room and leaving him; or you can bring your dog into an isolated area such as a crate or a bathroom and leave him there alone. I prefer the second but there are instances when the first is more effective. Time outs should last for no more than two minutes maximum but always start with thirty seconds. If your dog is ignored for too lengthy a period of time, he will simply forget what behavior caused this consequence and you will have taught him nothing.

Your timing is VERY important when doing a time out. The time out has to occur IMMEDIATELY following the offending behavior. You want your dog to associate that behavior with all attention being withdrawn. That is critical. Behaviors happen quickly, so if your timing is off, you could wind up punishing your dog for a good behavior like sitting. When doing time outs, use a marker word, like "Too Bad" or "Oops". It should be said in a sing song voice, not in an angry tone. There must not be any bad emotion in your acknowledgment of the behavior. Bad attention is still attention and a dog will continue to exhibit the behavior for any attention, good or bad.

For time outs to be effective, they must be consistent. For example, if your dog is barking in your face demanding your attention, you must implement the time out every time he barks at you. If you do it one time and the next time, you let it go you are sending a confusing signal to your dog. Typically, repeating the time out many times in even one day will make an impression on your dog as to what will happen if the unwanted behavior continues. It does get tiresome to keep doing it, but the more consistent you are in doing it, the faster your dog will understand.

Here are a few behaviors where time outs would be indicated

but this list is by no means all inclusive: dog barks demandingly for attention; dog play bites incessantly; dog jumps on people repeatedly; dog licks people excessively; dog constantly paws people for attention; dog behaves inappropriately with other dogs (for this, take the dog to a spot well away from the other dogs and remove his ability to play for the recommended time—this applies to resident dogs as well as visiting playmates); dog is being excessively active and exhibiting attention-seeking behavior.

A note on the barking issue: the only time you can waver on the timing rule is if your dog is still barking at the end of the time frame. If he is still barking when the time is completed, wait patiently for the moment that he stops and let him out IMMEDIATELY. So you want to be close by and if it seems that the barking won't ever stop, poke your head around so that he can see you. He will probably stop briefly, say "YES!" and rush to let him out. If he starts barking again, don't say anything and go back to where you can't be seen and only poke your head out when he quiets. It shouldn't take long after that.

Always reward heavily for appropriate behavior. The key to phasing out the need for excessive time outs is to always communicate to your dog what you want him to do as opposed to the inappropriate behavior that he is practicing. Give him options and reward for the appropriate choice!

TRAINING TREATS

At the end of this section I have provided the treat recipes that I use both for my dogs and my clients' dogs. However, I don't expect everyone to bake for their dogs. I am a realist. So here are several other options that you can utilize for High Value Treats:

- Boiled chicken
- Lean beef slivers
- Homemade treats that include hearty meats such as liver
- Peanut butter, the stickier the better. Natural peanut butter, although healthier, is runny. Use traditional peanut butter in this case

- Microwaved all-beef kosher hot dogs with a sprinkling of garlic powder (or any hot dogs if you don't care what is actually in them!)
- Tiny chunks of smelly cheese (go easy on the cheese quantity, as too much can cause constipation)
- Pre-packaged natural soft treats such as Wellness Wellbites®, Wellness Pure Rewards®, Zukes®, Plato®, etc. cut into even smaller pieces

I recommend staying away from brightly colored supermarket treats that are full of sugar and preservatives. This can be the equivalent of feeding your kids candy bars for dinner and expecting them to be calm afterwards. Read the labels on any training treats you contemplate buying. While many trainers will tell you to buy the training treats that are sold in a sausage-like roll, I tend to avoid those. While they are certainly not as bad as the above mentioned supermarket treats, they do contain large amounts of wheat as well as fructose. These are two things that I don't think dogs need and there are plenty of good quality soft treats out there so it's not necessary to use these products. Then why do I have whole wheat as an ingredient in my recipes? I personally use buckwheat flour as I am gluten intolerant as is Kera, my white princess. But I do not expect everyone to run out and buy buckwheat flour, which can be hard to find. If your dog is not sensitive to wheat or gluten, then by all means use whole wheat flour to bake these! But the difference between homemade treats based on my recipes, made with whole wheat flour and store bought training rolls is that the homemade treats do not contain sugar, which dogs definitely do not need! Any of the treats that I mention are meant to be cut into the tiniest of pieces.

And while biscuit-like treats are great for Kong® stuffing and showing appreciation for the happiness that your dogs give you, they are simply not high value enough to use as training treats. For one, they really are not as high value as say a piece of boiled chicken or a big lick of peanut butter. And the other downside is that they have to stop and chew the crunchy treats. Dogs don't multi-task as well as we do. All that crunching tends to make them forget what they got that biscuit for. So soft is better here. And with peanut butter, you get more bang for your buck, so to speak. While the treats that you hand out are eaten very quickly usually, with peanut butter, one good lick will result in quite a few seconds of mouth movement while trying to process that sticky mouthful! And it's hard to forget what caused that mouthful to be awarded to him. Win/win here!

So for all of you bakers who will cook for your dogs, here are some winners for you.

HOMEMADE LIVER BROWNIES CUT UP INTO TRAINING TREAT SIZE PIECES.

LIVER BROWNIES
- 1# beef liver (including the blood)
- 1 cup buckwheat or whole wheat flour
- 4 whole eggs (including shells)
- Generous sprinkling of garlic powder

1. Puree all up in a food processor or if you are using a blender, puree eggs and liver and transfer to a mixing bowl to add the flour.
2. Pour into a greased brownie sized pan.
3. Sprinkle generously with grated parmesan or shredded cheese.
4. Bake at 350 degrees for 20-25 minutes depending on your oven.
5. Let cool on rack before cutting.
   Your house will smell strongly of liver.

CHEESE BISCUITS

- 1 package (2 cups) of finely shredded cheddar or other type of shredded cheese
- 1/2 cup vegetable oil
- 2 cups buckwheat or whole wheat flour
- healthy shake of garlic powder

1. Mix very well in a large mixing bowl.
2. Add enough water to make a soft dough.
3. Roll out onto floured surface using enough flour on the dough to stop the sticking if you want to use cookie cutters like a bone shaped one.
4. Or you can just shape them into flattened balls. (Don't make them super thin)
5. Bake on a greased cookie sheet at 400 degrees for no more than 10 minutes, but check them at 8 if your oven runs hot.

SALMON BROWNIES

- 2 cans pink salmon or jack mackerel, undrained
- 4 whole eggs, shells and all
- healthy sprinkling of garlic powder
- 1 cup or so of grated parmesan cheese
- 2 to 3 cups buckwheat or whole wheat flour (depends on your preference)

Mix first four ingredients well in large bowl. Add flour at the rate of ½ cup at a time. If batter is still too moist at 2 cups, add more. Use your judgment. Batter should stick together but not be very moist. Grease two large cookie sheets well and press batter via a plastic spatula in a thin layer. It should not be so thin that there is pan showing through but you are not looking for real brownie thickness. It may not cover each sheet completely and that is normal. Sprinkle more parmesan on top if desired. Cook one at a time in a preheated 350 degree oven for approx. 30-40 minutes. Cool on rack and then use a pizza cutter to cut up. Freezes well.

Acknowledgements

This book has been in the making for longer than I imagined it would be. There have been many people during that time who have helped me in various ways. To not thank them properly would be unthinkable so here goes. They are in no particular order of importance as this has been a team effort for sure. I am terrified I will forget someone!

First off, I want to thank my publisher Pete Smoyer, for having the patience of Job with my scattered way of thinking and expressing myself. Sometimes all that energy simply doesn't come out as coherently as would be preferable. And thanks to Pete's super wife, dog trainer extraordinaire, Ali Brown, for suggesting Pete in the first place as well as for her wonderful proofreading skills.

Thanks to Leslie McDevitt for inspiring me to do this. Thanks to all the trainers who are my inspiration and whom I learned from in various venues; among them are the aforementioned Leslie and Ali, as well as Pat Miller, Pam Dennison, Suzanne Clothier, Dr. Patricia McConnell, Emma Parsons, and too many others to mention. In particular, Patricia McConnell's little booklet was the first place I turned to when I found myself with more dogs than I had planned. I learned first about multiple dog dynamics from her knowledge and foraged hungrily for more information from every possible source since then. This is the result of all my foraging.

Several clients have been very supportive of my efforts and one in particular really encouraged me early on. Susan Hudacheck, you are a dear. Thanks for your vision. You helped light the spark that became this book.

Another client also became a friend. And that friend turned out to be a professional copy editor. What luck! Thanks so much Michelle Belan, for your valuable input and support.

Many thanks to the trainers at Animal Friends shelter in Pittsburgh who noticed my talent with unruly dogs and nurtured it. Special thanks to Kathy Reck, Lilian Akin, Barb Grosch, Jan McCune and Lori Caruso. A couple of those mentioned also graciously permitted me to modify some of their training handouts for my own preferences. Thanks for not requiring me to reinvent the wheel!

There are so many people who helped me pull together photos for this project and I am eternally grateful for that. I never imagined how many photos one had to take and look through to select just a few! Babeth Raible and Crystal Collins-Johnson, I owe you both plenty! Without your fabulous pictures, this book would be much less entertaining. Grateful thanks also to Anne Walizer, Lilian Akin (again), Jennifer Matthews, Marci Gross, Jane Fratesi, Scott Bates and Polly Bray. And thanks to all of the wonderful dogs who modeled for the camera.

Thanks to all those who supplied their versions of real life solutions: Sue Kerr, Joy Kemmler, Joyce Petrow, Susan Hudacheck, Crystal Collins-Johnson, Lilian Akin, Chris Ros, Jennifer Matthews and Cheri Ludwick. Thanks also with much gratitude to Crystal Collins-Johnson and Carma Rey Klaja for lending their time and patience for proofreading

Thanks to my friends who were very supportive of my efforts to get this completed. I really appreciate it. Especially Lilian who supplied the laptop it was written on!

Thanks especially to my dogs, both past and present, for teaching me how to be a better person. Gone for now but never forgotten, Samantha, Layla and Damon were my personal lost loves. Dustin was one of my first foster dogs who taught me so much. I wish I could have helped him more than I did. My present crew, Merlin, Kera, Siri and Trent endured many hours of me glued to a computer endlessly begging them for a just a little longer so I could get this show on the road soon. Thanks for your patience with that and the endless modeling for the camera. I wish I could find a way to keep you all with me in this realm as long as I am here. You are all my teachers and my soul mates, especially my first boy dog Merlin.

Thanks to the universe and the higher powers for making this all possible. I hope I never let you down.

Debby McMullen

Glossary

Body Blocking: this entails placing your erect postured body between a dog and anything that needs energy directed away from it, be it another dog, a doorway, a person, etc. It also refers to walking between your dogs as a group to break up the energy of a situation that has the potential to escalate into something unpleasant.

Clicker: a plastic and metal device designed to be used as a marker signal to acknowledge appropriate and desired behavior. It signals to the dog that he just did something that is a very good thing. A clicker is meant to mean that a treat is imminent. The connection between the treat and the clicker creates the value of the clicker. The clicker is the highest value marker. It implies that a treat WILL follow the click 100% of the time. The clicker should never lie.

Compliance: any desired behavior. Compliance is achieving quality impulse control in as many different scenarios as possible. The extent of compliance that is important to be achieved is individual among owners. Compliance should result in rewards. Some behaviors should be unacceptable and worked towards extinction. Aggression is one of them.

Consequence: a result of the dog's actions whether they be positive or negative.

Criteria: the context of the situation as a whole. An example of this is a dog knowing a solid attention cue in the house. But when on a walk, the distractions are magnified, so lowering the criteria means accepting a slight turn in your direction and marking/rewarding that to build upon it. Raising the criteria would be moving that solid attention cue practice to a quiet yard.

Cue: a word or signal that activates a particular behavior in a dog. The verbal version is sometimes referred to as a command. I prefer cue. It has more positive connotations.

Impulse control: indicates that a dog can ignore his desires and respond to his owner's cues instead. Having good impulse control results in frequent compliance.

Kong®: a rubber toy that is designed to be stuffed with food to be extracted by your dog. A Kong can assist a dog relaxing in various scenarios, especially when home alone.

Marker word: a verbal signal used to do the same as a clicker. However, a verbal marker is not as high value as a clicker. It is not associated with a treat 100% of the time like a clicker is.

Nothing in Life is Free: a strict program that exchanges particular behaviors such as a sit or a down for every resource that a dog gets. Examples of this include meals, petting, going outside, etc. While it is important to establish guidelines and expectations in order to properly teach manners, it is important to not take this sort of thing to extremes."

Premack Principle: asking your dog to do something you want in order that he may be permitted to do something he wants. Example; your dog wants to sniff a particular spot, you require that he look at you and "ask", then permit him to sniff for a moment. It's the exchange of a low probability behavior for a higher probability behavior.

Proofing a behavior: training to a degree that a dog can respond to cues he knows, even in the presence of strong distractions. This is achieved in steps.

Reactivity: when a dog gets overly excited about any number of things that can appear in his environment. Signs of reactivity can include barking, whining, crying, lunging, snapping, etc. These can be both on leash only or on and off leash, both inside and outside the home. It is typically caused by fear, though it appears as aggression. The dog is acting preemptively to make the "scary" thing go away.

Socialize: exposing a dog to many different people, animals, objects and situations in order that he might be more comfortable no matter what transpires and less inclined to be suspicious or fearful.

Resources and References

BOOKS

Aggression: These books can assist with several types of aggression but are not a substitute for a professional behavior consultant.

Aloff, Brenda, *Aggression in Dogs: Practical Management, Prevention & Behavior Modification*, Dogwise Publishing, 2002.

Dennison, Pamela S., *How to Right a Dog Gone WRONG: a Roadmap for Rehabilitating Aggressive Dogs*, Alpine, 2005.

Parsons, Emma, *Click to Calm: Healing the Aggressive Dog,* Sunshine Books, 2005.

Behavior: Three of these books are not specifically about dogs but they are about behavior, which is universal. The first two listed can assist in learning to pay attention to your instincts which can help you manage a multiple dog household. The last one will reveal why using force is not advisable.

de Becker, Gavin, *The Gift of Fear: Survival Signals That Protect Us From Violence*, Little, Brown & Company, 1997.

Gladwell, Malcolm, *Blink: The Power of Thinking Without Thinking,* Little, Brown & Company, 2005.

Sidman, Murray, *Coercion and Its Fallout*, Authors Cooperative, 2000.

Body Language: These books can be very informative in teaching you how to "read" your dogs better.

Aloff, Brenda, *Canine Body Language: A Photographic Guide,* Dogwise Publishing, 2005, www.brendaaloff.com.

Handelman, Barbara, *Canine Behavior: A Photo Illustrated Handbook,* Woof and Word Press, 2008, www.dogtrainingathome.com.

Rugaas, Turid. *On Talking Terms with Dogs: Calming Signals.* 2006 Dogwise Publishing, 2006, www.turid-rugaas.no/UKFront.htm.

Cognitive and emotion information: These books discuss the emotional and cognitive understanding that dogs possess. They also discuss other species as well. Understanding this aspect of your dogs will give you an edge.

Bekoff, Marc, *The Emotional Lives of Animals,* New World Library, 2007, http://literati.net/Bekoff/.

Csanyi, Vilmos, *If Dogs Could Talk,* North Point Press, translated in 2005.

McConnell, Patricia, *For the Love of a Dog: Understanding Emotion in You and Your Best Friend,* 2007, www.dogsbestfriendtraining.com.

Feeding: These books will educate you about the raw food diet for dogs.

Johnson, Susan K., *Switching to Raw: A Fresh Food Diet for Dogs That Makes Sense,* 1998 Birchrun Basics, 1998, www.switchingtoraw.com.

Lonsdale, Tom, *Raw Meaty Bones Promote Health,* Rivetco P/L, Australia, 2001.

McDonald, Carina Beth, *Raw Dog Food: Make it Easy for You and Your Dog*, Dogwise Publishing, 2004.

General Positive Training: These books are handy general training references to have on hand.

Arden, Andrea, *Dog Friendly Dog Training,* Howell Book House, 2007, www.andreaarden.com.

Dennison, Pamela, *The Complete Idiots Guide to Positive Dog Training,* Alpine Books, 2006, www.positivedogs.com.

Miller, Pat, *Positive Perspectives: Love Your Dog Train Your Dog,* Dogwise Publishing, 2004.

Miller, Pat, *The Power of Positive Dog Training,* Wiley Publishing, 2001, www.peaceablepaws.com.

Pryor, Karen, *Don't Shoot the Dog: The New Art of Teaching and Training,* Bantam Books, 1999.

Multiple Dogs: This booklet is the original multiple dog resource.

London, Ph.D., Karen B. & McConnell, Ph.D., Patricia B., *Feeling Outnumbered? How to Manage and Enjoy Your Multi-Dog Household,* Dog's Best Friend, Ltd., 2001.

Reactivity: These books are important tools in modifying reactivity in your dog.

Brown, Ali, *Scaredy Dog! Understanding and Rehabilitating Your Reactive Dog,* Tanacacia Press, 2009, www.greatcompanions.info.

Dennison, Pamela, *Civilizing the City Dog: A Guide to Rehabilitating Aggressive Dogs in an Urban Environment.* Alpine Publications, 2007.

McDevitt, Leslie, *Control Unleashed: Creating a Focused and Confident Dog,* Clean Run Productions, 2007, www.controlunleashed.com.

Relationship Building: These books are life changing reads. You will be inspired.

Clothier, Suzanne, *Bones Would Rain from the Sky*, Warner Books, 2002, www.flyingdogpress.com.
McConnell, Patricia, *The Other End of the Leash: Why We Do What We Around Dogs,* Ballantine Books, 2002.

Scientific: The first book discusses the evolution of dogs. The second is intense but does contain the official version of the Relaxation Protocol. The unofficial versions of the RP can be obtained via a Google search.

Coppinger, Raymond and Lorna, *Dogs: A Startling New Understanding of Canine Origin, Behavior & Evolution,* Scribner, 2001.
Overall, Dr. Karen, *Clinical Behavioral Medicine for Small Animals*, Mosby, 1997.

DVDs

This is an excellent set to learn more body language moves from.

Kalnajs, Sarah, *The Language of Dogs:Understanding Canine Body Language and Other Communication Signals,* Blue Dog Training & Behavior, LLC., 2007, www.bluedogtraining.com.
Rugaas, Turid, *Calming Signals: What Your Dogs Tell You,* Dogwise, 2005.

Websites

www.apdt.com, Association of Pet Dog Trainers: Locate a dog trainer.
www.dogaware.com, Health and feeding info.
www.dogwise.com, Dog books and DVD's.
www.clickertraining.com, Karen Pryor's website.
www.iaabc.org, International Association of Behavior Consultant: Locate a behavior consultant.

www.K9rawdiet.com, Treats and chew products.
www.kongcompany.com, Kong products.
www.livescience.com/animals/070715_moon_pets.html,   full
moon study on dog and cat behavior.
www.petexpertise.com, Toys, treats, training accessories.
www.petfinder.com, Petfinder: Pet adoption resources.
www.rawfed.com; www.rawfeddogs.net; www.rawlearning.com;
www.rawmeatybones.com; Raw feeding information.
     www.trulydogfriendly.com, Truly Dog Friendly: Locating a dog
friendly trainer & information on positive training.

Calming Remedies:
Aromadog Chill Out Spray; www.aromadog.com
Bach Rescue Remedy®; www.rescueremedy.com
Bach Flower Essences®; www.bachflower.com/pets.htm
Comfort Zone® with D.A.P.® ; www.petcomfortzone.com

Management Tools:
Premier Products™: Gentle Leader™ Head Halter, Gentle Leader™ Easy Walk Harness, The Premier Collar™ (Martingale style), Calming Cap™, Tug-a-Jug™; www.premier.com[1]
Ruff Rider Roadie Car Safety Harness; www.ruffrider.com

Publications:
Whole Dog Journal: www.wholedogjournal.com
The Bark Magazine: www.thebark.com

---

1   As this book went to print, Premier Pet Products, LLC was purchased by Radio Systems Corporation. RSC is a manufacturer of shock collars of various kinds. I will no longer be purchasing or recommending Premier Products to my clients. If the situation changes and ownership by RSC changes, I will happily go back to supporting Premier Pet Products, LLC. I felt it important to advise readers of this situation.

Index

Photo Credits

Lilian Akin 56, 78, 84

Crystal Collins-Johnson 20, 37(both), 52, 57, 58, 102, 109, 110(top), 114(top and middle),

Jane Fratesi 113(bottom)

Marci Gross 112(top)

Jennifer Matthews 39, 119, 142

Debby McMullen 22, 23, 24, 26, 30, 38, 47, 53, 54, 60, 86, 93, 97, 187

Babeth Raible 21, 31, 36, 79, 90, 110(bottom), 111, 113(top), 114(bottom), 115(both), 117, 118

Anne Walizer 8, 112(bottom)